THE GREEK GODS

an iconoclast's guide

To all Celts in the Diaspora, and to Iconoclasts everywhere.

And most especially in both memory of, and in honour to, all the Heroic Prometheans of the S.C.

With special thanks to the following for their inspiration and humour:

Virgil; Aristophanes; Catullus; Lucian; and Thalia the Muse of Comedy.

Maureen O'Sullivan

THE GREEK GODS

an iconoclast's guide

EFSTATHIADIS GROUP

Efstathiadis Group S.A.
Agiou Athanasiou Street,
GR - 145 65 Anixi, Attikis

ISBN 960 226 048 3

Printed and bound in Greece by Efstathiadis Group S.A.

This book is intended as a manual of instruction for all Tourists in the Greek World who have forgotten all *their Classical Mythology, or, who in point of fact, never received* any *to forget — in the first place!*

Throughout the Greek World you will find the ruins of temples, see the remnants of the Ancient Civilization, and hear references to the 'Greek Gods'! It really seems that if you don't know something about these Gods, then you will be missing out on the whole Greek Experience, and that is why this book is written.

But, this book is written by an Iconoclast. The Writer believes in the existence of the Gods in our lives, but she does not worship them. That is why this is a slightly different interpretation of the Gods, and is possibly the first time they have been pulled down so low from the lofty heights of Olympus — to be seen in their true light — simply as Men — not, as Deities.

The deification exists solely in our minds, as we mortals are the ones who made them Gods in the first place.

The first part of this book is meant for the enlightenment of the Reader — the second part is for sheer entertainment.

The Reader may feel free to completely skip the 'enlightenment' if he, or, she so wishes, and just get on with enjoying him/herself.

A little laughter never hurt anyone, whereas a little enlightenment often did!

5

The Family Tree of the Principal Gods

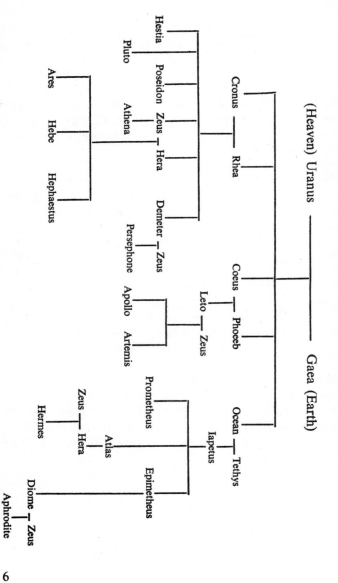

Contents

The Birth of Religious Desire in Man, "There *must* be Someone
Running This Show!"

CHAPTER I

WHY AND HOW MAN INVENTED THE GODS

The Birth of the Primitive Religious Form.

When the first men looked around on earth, and saw what a rotten place it was, and how miserably men behaved to each other; then they must have said to themselves, "What a confounded mess! There must be *Something Better* than this! And there must be *Someone Better* than us! And there must be *Someone Running This Show,* who will try and bring some sort of *Order* and *Justice* and *Logic* to this catastrophic situation which we call *LIFE!*

With this desire and despair was born the *Myth of the Gods!*

Early man invented the Gods because he had a tremendous need of them! A need to have some Super-Being to whom he could pray, and to whom he could give respect and adoration. A Super-Creature who would help him in this life, and possibly give him some sort of comfort and future in the *"Next"*. *(Not* that early man was convinced that there was a *Next Life* – but he was hopeful, as well as insecure and fearful!)

Of course the animals didn't need to worry about such things. They simply got on with living, and had no doubts about the future. In this respect they were more fortunate than man – who couldn't enjoy his life for fear of what would happen when it ended; and who had trouble making sense of all the ugliness and unnecessary suffering which he was continually enduring at the hands of his fellow man (not to mention the earthquakes, floods, droughts and other natural disasters which were also continually and relentlessly over-taking him).

Man needed a Being which would be All Perfect, All Knowing, and All Stable. A Being, or Beings, on which he could depend, and which would supply some type of *Reason,* for all the *Unreasonableness* which surrounded him.

So, along came the Poet, or early Idealist and Dreamer; the man to supply to others a picture of perfection, and to create a person, or persons, who neither hungered, nor sorrowed, and indeed never suffered as man did.

This Poet was a man of imagination; a spinner of tales; a man who sang of things *NOT* as they were – but as they *SHOULD BE!*

He drew different deities, showing wondrous details in the world which had not been noticed before, and he created the Gods in beautiful imagery, and served up this dream to the people; in order to comfort them.

The people then ate the fruit of their dreams, and the resultant indigestion was entirely their own fault – after all, they had ordered the dish in the first place!

The Poet was the original God-Maker, and with his stories, and phantastic myths and dreams he supplied a product for which there was a tremendous market – thus satisfying a fundamental need in the people.

Hot on the heels of the Poet, came the Manipulator, or Power-Hungry Man. He realised that by controlling these dreams and myths, he could more easily control the people themselves, and thereby have more Power, more Land, more Slaves, and above all – *Consolidate His Position More Firmly in the Tribe!*

Sometimes this Manipulator and Realist was the Head-Man, or the Priest – or even a group of Elders and Priests. These pragmatists took the songs and *stories* of the Poets, and the *needs* of the People, and fashioned them both to suit their *own aims.*

The early 'Establishment' said to itself, "So they want Gods! Well, let them have them! But, make them in *Our Image,* and put *Our Words* into their mouths, because then it will be a lot easier for us to control them through these Gods!

So the *Exploitation of the Myth Was Born!*

Because the Mythology was now in the hands of the 'Establishment', it began to change and take on a new character to suit those in power. That is why in the mythological stories there are some differences of opinion; some versions which are widely disparate in their views of events and people. The Gods have characters which change with the history of the State itself. Old Gods are overthrown, and New Gods replace them; – and the whole power struggle takes place through the medium of phantasy.

Originally all primitive peoples invented their Gods from the materials of Nature, because their world was an extremely physical one, and was controlled by the forces of this Nature which they could not comprehend.

The first God to appear was generally the Sun, because it furnished light, heat, and life itself to these poor primitives, and its power was perceived to be of supernatural strength, even to their dim understanding.

After the Sun, came the Moon; which was the other side of their life; representing the mysterious, frightening night (possibly also representing Death) and this Moon they could no more account for, than the Sun. And what one cannot account for (or understand) always arouses a sense of awe and respect.

In the mind of the primitive man, the Sun became associated with masculine strength, and ferocious heat, and anger; and the Moon symbolised cool femininity, and peace, and love – plus a small dash of terror for good measure!

The winds, the sea, the rivers, the trees; all became Super Natural Spirits, due to their being indispensable to life; and due to their not being fully understood and comprehended. So the very earth itself, and the skies above it, took on the characteristics of Deities – because of the need of these first hunting and agricultural people to survive in this world with which they daily battled in order to wrest a livelihood.

Certain animals which were scarce became sacred, and therefore had to be spared (Supply and Demand) while others which were evil, or else considered a source of strength, had to be killed and eaten in order to gain this strength.

The hunter also thought to bribe the Spirits by paying tribute to them with donations or offerings from his 'game', as these early deities were not considered generous beings, but rigid autocrats; who demanded their just dues from man.

Mother Earth herself would not yield large quantities of grain and other crops unless her thirst for expiation had been appeased. "You can't take from Nature without paying back!" the early farmer said, and the modern farmer knows that scientifically this is actually correct.

This early idea of sacrificing, in order to win the approval of the various Spirits and Gods, was naturally encouraged by the Tribal Manipulators, who used it as another means of keeping power over the people.

And this early form of 'Fertilization' of the land, by cutting the throat of some unfortunate, and allowing his or her blood to seep into the earth to feed it mineral and protein, proved quite effective. Nowadays modern farmers, beside using chemical manure, occasionally plough back their crops in order to feed the soil, which is basically the same principle. They are simply returning to Mother Nature some food, in order to re-pay her for all the nourishment they have taken from her. (Incidentally, at the time of the Crimean War, 1854–56, British farmers actually used the ground bones of dead soldiers from that sorry conflict in order to fertilize their acres. The history books do not bother to elaborate on whether they happened to be British, Russian, Turkish, French or Sardinian ground bones. But the moral of the tale seems to be that nothing beats Human Sacrifice for a good crop harvest!)

The manipulators however, decided to put this primitive form of Fertilization to better use than as a mere agricultural incentive. They saw that Human Sacrifice was a means of: –

1. Population Control in the Tribe (in view of the fact that they didn't have the modern methods of Contraception which we enjoy today).

2. Liquidation of Rebellious Elements in the Tribe (our modern form of this, is Capital Punishment!)

3. Satisfaction of the Tribal Members, and an outlet for all their Frustrations (we generally arrange Blood Sports, Athletic Meetings, and Sport-Car Racing nowadays.)

4. Intimidation of Discontented Tribal Members (the Primitives didn't have the elaborate Prison System which we have.)

5. Consolidation of the Power of the Rulers (for this aspect, we use the Press and the Law in general.)

6. Re-enforcement of the Ritual Aspects of Religion (still in use today!)

So Human Sacrifice came to be an accepted ritual in religion, although later, money and gifts would be used in place of actual people. Human Beings were sacrificed in the various wars anyway, and War itself achieved all the above objects of the Manipulators.

The Birth of the City and Formalized Religion.

As men became more civilized and towns were built, there came a need for Temples to be erected, and for a more constitutionalized religious form to be implemented.

New Gods came into being, and the Priests tusselled with the Elders of the tribe and the Landowners, in order to gain supreme power in this new period of Man's Evolution.

The Priests finally opted to become the subtle, inauspicious rulers of the people and became the 'King-Makers'; for as 'Holy Men', *ONLY THEY* could correctly interpret the commands and dictates of the Divine Beings, and hand their messages on to the people. The Priests had *Power without seeming to have it,* and in consequence were therefore *much more Powerful!*

The Religion began to constitute the Law of the Land, and the Leaders (via the Priests) ruled with 'Divine Authority'. The Gods themselves took on more sophisticated forms in answer to

13

the needs of progress, so the old Vegetation Deities like Mother Earth and her crops, and the Natural Forces of Nature like the Sun, and the Moon, gave way to new Gods formed in the shape of Mortal Men; who bore a strong resemblance to the upper echelons of the society.

These Gods were useful also in that they served a specific purpose in the schemes of the State, and were occupied with certain necessary functions such as: – the **God of War,** or the **Goddess of Love,** or the Chief God of All – who, by his very existence and presence, gave substance and authority, and a beautiful sense of calm control to the newly born civilized society.

Some religions in various societies of the Far East and the Middle East also invented a type of early 'Devil', or 'Bad God', to which everything adverse could be attributed; while others thought to invent Gods which were half men, and thereby give the mortal worker and the slave more inducement and motivation to worship the Immortals of the State Religion (which Religion happened to be the Code of Conduct and Set of Laws for the newly emerging Nation.)

Whenever there was a change in society, and new Gods were needed to replace the old, or to keep pace with the times, the Poets always supplied these Deities – thus giving birth to Literature in its earliest form of Mythology.

As the philosopher **Hegel** said, "Religion is the sphere in which a nation gives itself a definition of that which it regards as the True". What Hegel omitted to mention was exactly who defined this 'Truth' – the people themselves – or their Leaders?

Mythology, which always supports Religion, therefore helps to control the minds of men. But Man himself, is inevitably hoisted on his own mythological petard, because although originally, he (Man) gave shape to the Gods – eventually these Gods themselves, began to give shape to Man's mind!

The Ancient Gods of the Ancient Greeks, before the City-States began arising around 800 B.C. were like those of other primitive peoples, and were the early Gods of the Peasants. They were Physical Gods, Deities of Nature, like Mother Earth and Father Sun. Gods which had a direct meaning for them, and a tangible impact on their lives.

But from the time the Barons of Thessaly in Greece began to build an Aristocracy, and to construct new cities; took to indulging in commerce; began conquering other peoples, and setting up a complicated system of Classes and Slavery; then the primitive Nature Gods began to be vanquished by a new cast of characters and personalities called the **"Olympians"** (who appropriately enough lived above Thessaly where the Barons dwelt). These new Gods had all the characteristics, and even the facial features, of the early nobility who ruled the first City-States.

The Story of the banishment of the Old Primitive Gods, and the coming of the New Olympian Gods as set out in the Greek Mythology, is in fact, the history of the commencement of the establishment of the Greek City-States, and the early Greek Empire.

All Mythology is a form of History, and all History is a form of Mythology. As Napoleon said, "What is History, but a fable agreed upon".

The Myth is a lie, based on a small modicum of truth; and it is the glamourised version of what someone, somewhere, wishes the true facts had *really been!*

WHERE DID THE GREEK GODS COME FROM?

The Greek Gods originally came from all over the Middle Eastern World. They were originally derived from various religious myths and ideas which had been circulating in India, Egypt, Summaria, Babylon, Phoenica, Persia, Mycenai, Crete and Troy.

The Olympian Gods of the Ancient Greeks were simply the combinations – the mixtures of stories and ideas – which the

Greeks had acquired, while on their journeys through the many lands they traversed until they reached their final settlements around the Mediterranean and Aegean Seas.

These Gods were also formed as a result of the various tales which they had heard from the lips of strangers passing through their new Greek ports.

These Gods had characteristics based on innumerable diverse aspects of other older civilizations, but as the Greeks came at a later stage in Civilization itself, i.e. the Historic Evolutionary Civilization of the World, so too they were more advanced in many different fields than the other centres of civilization in the East had been. Therefore their Gods and their State Religious System were more advanced as well, and so this State System has survived and endured with us right down to the present day.

The Greeks 'institutionalised' religion, and created a system of Gods who were almost perfect in their suitability for every strata of the Society, and they were Gods who spoke with the voice of the *State,* and *not* the voice of the **Priest.** Under the Greeks, the Priests became subservient to *the State,* and merely interpreted the Gods in order to *please the Rulers.*

The Greek Gods of Olympus were 'National' Gods, and kept the 'Status Quo' upholding the power of the Ruling Class. They embodied all the moral concepts of the Greek Rulers, and were the Spokespeople for the Political System, and the inspiration for all the endeavours of the Greek people themselves. They symbolised *Order, Justice,* and *Beauty,* and were extremely nationalistic, as were the Greeks themselves, who guarded their citizenship very jealously.

The Greek State Religion was born in Olympus in the clouded mountains above the plains of Thessaly where the new agricultural aristocracy lived. These new agricultural nobles of Greece, soon to become rich merchants, and educated and sophisticated denizens of the new City-States, had learnt from observing the mistakes of the Pharoes, *not* to allow the Priest to hold full sway in the Society. So the Greek Gods came under their *exclusive patronage,* and spoke and acted as they themselves would have.

As Greece expanded, and her 'life-style', became more complex, so too did her Gods become more formalized, and only the country people were left with their old Vegetation Myths to satisfy their hungry hearts and minds, as the City dwellers of Greece had turned to worship more sophisticated deities in keeping with their new professions and occupations.

There were twelve main Olympian Gods, and they typified every area of City-State life. There were deities for **Soldiers, Lovers, Educationists, Artists, Artisans** and **Metal Workers, Sailors, Hunters,** and married Women. There was also a god for the Dying, the Disabled, and the Spinster working in the home; not forgetting that most important being, the deity for Commerce and all Business Men; and the Chief Deity himself, **Zeus,** who, by his leadership, symbolized the complete Hierarchical System.

Originally, the Olympian Gods were the children of the Poets **Homer, Pindar,** and **Hesiod;** but the characters of the Gods themselves (and the idea of them as separate interesting deities) inspired many more to write about them, and they served as subjects for the Playwrights **Aeschlyus, Sophocles, Euripides** and **Aristophanes.**

The Gods came to mean the essence of all that was Greek, and of everything that meant Hellas and the Greek Spirit.

Poems and plays were written concerning their exploits. Wars were waged for them (or at least so it was said!) People were killed, songs were sung, statues and temples were built – and *All — For Them!*

The intellect of the Greek people was completely gripped in single-minded devotion to them, and the Greek Civilization System functioned completely under the Dictatorship of the **Olympians!**

The Gods were all beautiful, rich, and sensuous people, and they, like the mortals who controlled them, came from Good

Homer, 150 B.C.

Families! They were born blest, and superior, and it was right that they should be so.

According to the legends, sometimes a hard-working slave or worker had the chance to feast his eyes on these immortals, but generally only because he'd spent the better part of his existence with his eyes securely fixed on the ground; and with his soul securely ingrained in the knowledge of his own baseness and unworthiness. The Gods belonged to the Beautiful – and to the Rich!

THE IMPORTANCE OF THE GREEK GODS IN THE WESTERN WORLD

The Ancient Greeks invented the God Systen and Institutionalised Religion, but when the Romans conquered the Greeks in the Second Century B.C., they lifted the entire system; changed the names of the Gods to more fitting Latin ones; and adopted them to suit themselves.

Today, most of the **Greek Gods** are more familiarly known by their Roman names, and few realise where they came from initially. This migration of myths and religions is also true of Royalty (the Gods after all were Royal Symbols of Authority) as most Monarchs originally came from somewhere else, to rule over a people in an entirely different land; and once their names had been changed, then no one was any the wiser. Mythology, Monarchy, and Money, have *No Nationality!*

The Roman Gods are the Greek Gods. Old wine in new bottles, so to speak. The Romans built upon the Greek civilization and consolidated it, expanding it, and making more concrete, the general abstract ideas which they found flourishing in the City-States they had invaded.

Being a practical people, the Romans built roads and bridges and passed laws, and set-up colonies. Not being very imaginative however, they were forced to steal the Gods which they couldn't invent for themselves!

This is quite understandable when one considers the fact that the Romans, being more economically developed than the Greeks, were consequently extremely busy, and occupied in making money, and stealing other peoples' property! (It must be observed that it is seldom that one sees the average merchant spending the time to sit down and write a book, or compose a tune. The Business Man is a practical being, and has more important things to do than *Dream.* But as a *Realist,* he does recognise an opportunity when he sees it, and he knows quite well how to make money out of *other people's Dreams!)*

They Romans might have been among the first to steal a culture or a religion in such an open fashion, but they were not the last. The **Anglo-Saxons** also swiped the early stories of the **Celts** in pre-Anglo-Saxon Britain, and simply re-drew them to suit themselves. (To give but one example, King Lear in Shakespeare, is actually Lir, from the "Children of Lir", a story in Irish Mythology). So we find that to the Romans, **Eros** became **Cupid, Aphrodite** – **Venus,** and **Zeus himself** was re-named Jupiter.

At the beginning of the Roman rise to power, they produced no writers of any merit among themselves, as they were mostly soldiers and merchants, and therefore had to use Greeks in their homes as tutors, to teach them the niceties of civilization.

The also used the services of **Celtic poets** from Cis-Alpine Gaul, like Virgil and Catullus, to sing the praises of their mighty empire with idolatrous rubbish such as this, "Rome, loveliest Queen of all the World, Mother of Men, and Mother of the Gods".

So **Virgil,** the Celt from Gaul, wrote, in order to appease his imperial master Augustus, in Rome. But Rome was neither the 'Mother of Men', nor the 'Mother of the Gods', as she had stolen all these deities and fashioned them to suit herself (along with the lands of the vanquished Greeks) and then used this culture to promote the 'Pax Romana'.

When the Romans had begun to use the Celts in their empire

to pen their poetry, and when they had even developed a few writers of their own (by the beginning of the First Century A.D.) they were able to forsake the services of their Greek teachers to some extent.

By the time this began to happen, they were of course on their downward path of descent into their final historic oblivion. A society which produces many great and true artists is not a successful one, because Great Art, like everything else Great, is born in misery, and nutured by suffering; and merchants who begin to appreciate poetry, are beginning to lose their grip! The Spiritual World only attracts – when the Physical one is found lacking!

The Zenith of any society is actually its Nadir. It is in fact, the very point at which the 'Upward Incline' ends, and the 'Decline' begins!

In Greece, during the Athenian Supremacy, at the time of **Pericles** in the Fifth Century B.C., the Gods rose to their greatest position of power, and as the official theatre came into existence for the first time, the State took on the onerous task of indoctrination through spectacle.

(Later, the Romans would do the same thing in a slightly less edifying way, by the use of Gladiators and animals fighting in the arenas of the Colosseums).

The Greek theatre was born from the Myth; and the Greek State Religion, and Greek Literature is indebted to it.

These early theatres were supported by the State, and run on institutional lines, because they were the most efficient means of distributing the State Propaganda to a large number of people.

The Gods spoke with the State's Voice, and the early writers wrote with the State's Stylus; but somewhere along the way, the writers began to put their own personal words into the mouths of these Gods.

Euripides began to use the Gods to criticize the State, while Aristophanes made fools of the Gods, and of the people who formed his audience.

21

Portrait of Pericles, 440 B.C., Roman copy

When this began to happen, it demonstrated that the 'System' in Athens, and the other City-States in Greece (excluding the Spartans – who had given up the Arts entirely!) was in fact, only a hair's breath from extinction. Laughter has always been a weapon which dispels the power of Leaders. It also disipates the energies and the anger of the masses, which is why the 'System' has learnt to use this weapon of laughter *for itself.*

The Gods themselves, couldn't have liked what was happening, and must have been quite relieved to see the Romans conquer Greece, knowing then, that they could leave for Rome, where they would be worshipped in a more fitting manner (by people from good families!) and be taken seriously again!

It was important that the Gods be taken seriously because the Mythology, the Theatre, and the Religion were all working for the State; and for the State System of control and order.

Philosophers like Socrates were condemned to death simply because as non-believers in the Mythological System, they represented a threat to the people behind the Gods, i.e. the Manipulators, or Controllers.

In point of fact **Socrates** never actually neglected going to the Temples to sacrifice to the Gods in public (as was commanded by Law) but he *sinned in thought, if not in deed,* and therefore was a danger which had to be removed. *Seeming to believe was not enough!*

The Enemies of the Gods

Philosophy, War-Fatigue, and general disillusionment in Greece, led to the downfall of the Greeks, and to the abdication of their Gods.

The Sophists, who were around at the same time as Socrates (although he did not agree with their thinking at all!) were also deemed dangerous, as their philosophy maintained that *it really didn't matter one way or another if people believed in anything or not!*

Socrates 469-399 B.C.

Euripides, 340 B.C., Roman copy   *Sophokles,* 496-406 B.C.

This type of doctrine could hardly be expected to encourage people to go gladly off to wars, to fight for the Gods of their Cities, and the Homes of their Rulers!

But after undergoing a period of persecution, the Sophists explained that really they were not 'Anti-Gods', but simply people sitting on the fence observing the passing charade; and as such they were not giving the mass of people an alternative thought to follow, and therefore could not be a form of new subversive movement – or even constitute a minor threat to the State.

Having stated their case thus, they were (like most academics and artists everywhere) warmly welcomed back into the 'System' to provide a new 'non-Dangerous' Club for the disillusioned and disenchanted intellectuals of Athens.

Concurrent with, or slightly prior to this period of Religious Persecution, the Athenian State had decided to appear more 'Democratic' (for after all it was a Greek idea, and meant that one person in every twenty of the population had a vote!) and they finally allowed the emergence of complaint and criticism in the theatre. This is why Euripides was able to voice his eternal questions regarding the injustice of the Gods i.e. the System!

It is interesting to note that Euripides was able to pose almost the same questions in dramatic form, as Socrates was posing in philosophical form in the market place of Athens. Perhaps the moral of this is that it isn't so much *what you say, but the way that you say it!*

"Why?" asked Euripides continually. "Why are these people, these deities so bad? And why do we worship them if they are evil? And why, if we Greeks are such glorious people, have we done such terrible things to others?"

The Athenian crowds listened and watched, cried a little sentimentally into their handkerchieves (and thoroughly enjoyed this emotion, because sentimentality is an extremely pleasant experience to the dull and the selfish, constituting a type of Moral 'Compensation' for them!) and then retired to their homes – to eat their dinners – and to beat their slaves!

However it was Aristophanes and his comedies which finally deposed the Gods; held them up to ridicule for all to see; and by so doing, *took their power from them.*

Being satirized is a wearisome experience and so the Gods had already become exhausted with Greece, and were ready and waiting to leave for Rome when the Centurions came marching in.

In point of fact, they had packed their bags many years before!

Olympus – Residence of the Gods. "Off Limits to *all Mortals*!"

CHAPTER II

THE OLYMPIAN FAMILY

Greek Name	Roman Name	Occupation
Zeus	Jupiter	Captain of Gods
Poseidon	Neptune	God of the Sea
Hades/Pluto	Pluto/Dis	God of the Underworld
Hestia	Vesta	Goddess of the Hearth/Home
Hera	Juno	Goddess of Marriage/ Married Women
Ares	Mars	God of War
Athena	Minerva	Goddess of Education/ Science
Apollo	Apollo	God of Sun/Truth/Arts
Artemis	Diana	Goddess of Wild Things/ Chief Huntswoman
Aphrodite	Venus	Goddess of Love/Beauty
Hermes	Mercury	God of Commerce
Hephaestus	Vulcan	God of the Forge/Fire

The Olympian Family. "A typical evening at home in the White House."

Zeus

Zeus, the Captain of the Gods was a 'Big Daddy' type character who not only had the problems of the world to worry about, but also had continual strife in his own family to contend with.

Olympus itself was like some type of rich family mansion in the 'Deep South' with petty and pathetic intrigues erupting endlessly, and Zeus trying vainly to hold his power over the perfidious mortals below, while wasting most of his time in battle to maintain peace among the jealous, squabbling deities of his own house-hold!

Unfortunately for him, the Captain of the Gods suffered from an over-active pituitary gland which caused his Male Hormones to be in a constant state of extreme agitation. Zeus seemed to be a man continually combatting the depression of 'Male Meno-pause' and repeatedly trying to prove his virility, by seducing as many mortal and immortal females as possible!

The greater part of his time was not actually taken up in Government at all, but in running around on Earth, picking up maidens – ravishing them – and them running off before his wife could catch him!

Hera, his long suffering wife, also happened to be his sister, and this probably accounts for a great deal of the acrimony between them. After all, how many men *really get along with their sisters?* A wife is something which a man may find difficult enough to deal with, but a wife who is also a sister, is even more of a pain in the neck!

Marriage with Hera had obviously never been a love match anyway, but rather a political, economic alliance, formed at the time of the war between himself and Cronus when Zeus took over the world (see the Creation Story) so Zeus never felt particularly attracted to Hera in the physical sense!

Zeus symbolises the many men of substance and power in the early Greek society, who married in the interests of power, and contented themselves (sexually speaking) with something on the side. But in Zeus' case he was not content with a *little something* but wanted to eat out *all the time!*

Hera was very typical of the ever-vigilant wife, mindful of her interests, and never giving Zeus a quiet moment to pursue his peccadillos in peace. No matter where Zeus went, on land, or sea (or even up in the clouds) Hera was there soon after, nagging and scolding, and beating him over the head with her broom. (Olympian house-wives didn't use rolling-pins to beat up their husbands, because being immortal they didn't have to eat, and therefore never did any cooking.)

As he was the chief God and Leader, this hen-pecking routine began to get Zeus down, which is probably why he turned so nasty on all mortals who offended him, or indeed with anybody, anywhere, who attempted to undermine his authority. Deep in his heart Zeus knew that he was *NOT* the master in his own house, and this feeling of inferiority and suppressed rage made him a vicious bully when dealing with those weaker than himself.

Besides being constantly scolded by Hera, Zeus had a troublesome anarchistic uncle named Prometheus, who wanted to give away the secrets of power, and thereby help the *'Mob'* to take over.

Zeus tried to reason with him by saying, "You just don't understand the world and how things work! If *I* didn't have the power, then *somebody else would,* and things might be a lot *worse!* Anyway, I don't know why you're complaining, I give you power as well. Why don't you just relax and enjoy yourself? You're not even a mortal, so why are you worrying about them?"

But Prometheus kept carping on about the Revolution, and how they should build a Utopian society, and Zeus finally had to imprison him in order to get any rest.

Zeus carrying off infant *Ganymedes*

Apart from the trouble with Prometheus, Zeus was always under attack from the Old Gods, whose lands and power he had usurped. And to add to the bitterness of his lot, the Palace was full of chattering Muses, giggling Graces, and sundry children from his diverse amours!

Zeus

Like all families, the Olympians were rent by perpetual friction, and voices were continually raised for Zeus to award justice in the various disputes. The Chief of the Gods however, preferred pleasure to arbitration, and took to Earth in search of sexual diversion every time the duties of his office became too onerous.

As Hera was always spying on him, Zeus had to keep changing form, and so was often found on earth in the shape of a bull, or a tree, or an eagle (or in fact any other thing which just happened to be near some sweet young girl who was walking alone, and unaware in the woods!)

Childhood of *Zeus*

Naturally this constant need for metamorphosis, plus the constant fear of detection led Zeus to develop all sorts of internal complaints and psycho-somatic illnesses, which he exhibited by throwing around his thunderbolts, striking the earth with flashes of lightning, and sending large bursts of bad weather into the world.

During particularly stormy nights, the inhabitants of Athens would chortle and say, "Ah, yes! Hera must have caught him at his old tricks today. He's in a *terrible* mood tonight. Just listen to him, banging and thumping around up there!"

So it can be seen that Zeus never really commanded respect from anyone – only fear and derision. Exactly why the Eagle should have been chosen as his symbol is a bit of a mystery – unless of course that bird is *a secret coward also!*

Hera

Hera, as the wife of the Captain of the Gods, held a position similar to that of 'First Lady' of Olympus.

She thoroughly enjoyed her position as a source of power, but she did not enjoy being married to Zeus and having to spend her time trying to keep him away from other women.

Hera had originally been brought up by the **Titans Ocean** and Tethys, and as Zeus' sister she probably realised from the start that marriage to Zeus would be no bed of roses. However, she chose to dedicate herself and her entire time to the protection of all married women, and to persecute any women with whom Zeus dallied, or indeed, *any women anywhere — with whom any man dallied!*

She was extremely conservative, and lacking in any type of feminine allure, which is why she jealously hated all the other Goddesses in Olympus, and particularly loathed all the bastards – which Zeus filled up the house with! She tried her utmost to kill any of the children emanating from any of Zeus' love affairs, but he generally tricked her in some way or other, and managed to bring them home to Olympus for her to look after and educate.

One can almost sympathise with her over this point of etiquette, for how many women would like to have to bring up their husband's love children?

Not, mind you, that Hera was exactly chained to the housework, as she hardly did any, and all the affairs of Olympus and the running thereof, were left to her sister Hestia, who was the 'Old maid' of the family, and who might therefore think herself *lucky* to be a general dog's body, and slave, in such an illustrious establishment!

Hera also had her own little flings on the side, because her son Hephaestus is rumoured *not to have really been fathered by Zeus,* and her daughter Illithyia (Eileithyia) is likewise not accounted for in the family tree. **Eileithyia** incidentally, became the patron of all women in childbirth but never merited much of a mention

Zeus and *Hera*

in Mythology. Her name in modern form is Eileen, and she may be found in abundance in Ireland nowadays, as the Celts (who were always messing around in the Greek and Roman Empires) adopted a lot of the Greek Gods and Greek names, and took them with them to Erin. Even Patrick, that most Irish of names, is actually Greek, and means the 'Patriot' or the 'One who is Patriotic and who comes from the Country'. The word 'Patrida' is Greek for Country or Nation.

Mercury and *Hercules* protecting *Hera* from *Satyrs*

But enough of this etymology, and back to Hera!

Argos in Greece was the favourite city of Hera, and the peacock and the cow were both symbols of her authority. The peacock was supposed to contain the eyes of one of her erstwhile spies, whom she had once sent to watch over Zeus; and the cow was supposed to be representative of Hera herself, who is described (rather unfortunately) as 'cow faced'.

No wonder Hera had a massive complex about the infidelity of men – even the poets were less than gallant in penning lines in honour of her!

Zeus and *Hera* on the left, *Athena Poseidon* and *Mercury* on the right.

Bronze krater found at Derveni, third or second century B.C. Saloniki, Museum.

Poseidon

Poseidon the God of the Sea, was a younger brother of Zeus and it was from Zeus that Poseidon had secured his title and area of control. (Like all Mediterraneans, Zeus liked to keep things in the 'family' – a typical mafia trait also!)

Poseidon kept one Palace beneath the sea (an extremely magnificent affair with mermaids, sprites, and nymphs gambolling all around the place) but preferred to spend most of his time up in Olympus itself.

Poseidon and *Amphitrite*

As he was such an absentee landlord, the sea was continually getting out of control, and the sailors had to sacrifice either humans *or* animals in order to get any attention from Poseidon, and force him to come down and see to his domain. Mythology is full of stories about ship-wrecks which could easily have been

38

Poseidon talking to *Amphitrite*

avoided if only Poseidon hadn't been tearing around elsewhere and indulging himself in orgies!

He is supposed to have had come connection with bulls, but then practically all the Gods had some connection with bulls, and this only goes to show their original humble agricultural beginnings long before the development of the Greek City-States, which made both the Greeks and the Gods into Instant New Aristocrats! (But then all the aristocrats in the world had their humble origins in peasantry and land, which is how they developed their power in the first place!) Probably Poseidon, like most 'nouveau riche', didn't like to be reminded of his roots in the cow-shed, and so he only layed claim to giving the 'Horse' to the world. Horse-racing after all is the sport of Kings, and definitely on a higher social level than Bulls or Cows!

Poseidon was also called the **Earth-Shaker** because of his disagreeable habits, and was not particularly liked by any of the other Gods or Goddesses except Hera. He upset most of the occupants of Olympus, by trotting around

Poseidon and *Apollo.*

Poseidon fighting Giants.

40

The Big Three Super Powers. "A top notch Mafia Outfit"

with his trident in his hand, and sticking it into anyone with whom he happened to be conversing. He could not really be described as a 'Popular God', as the early Greeks thoroughly detested both the sea and him, and only became a nation of sailors very reluctantly.

Persephone abducted by *Plouto*

Hades/Pluto

Hades, or Pluto, was another brother of Zeus, and he was not nly the God of the Underworld, but also the **God of Wealth.** (This is hardly surprising when one thinks about it, for aren't most Funeral Directors and Mortury Owners wealthy men?) They have a sure-market we might say!

He was actually the King of Death, and not Death itselt, who was Thanatos, and whom the Romans called Orcus. But as the Chief Undertaker as it were, he had enormous wealth and power, especially during wars – and Greece *always had some war going on somewhere!* It seemed that the Greeks really liked giving him business, because if boring old peace seemed to threaten their lives for an instant, why the Spartans and Athenians would jump up and begin merrily bashing away at each other, in order to restore the usual comfortable, bloodthirsty life they all knew and loved so well.

Persephone and *Hades*

Pluto was also rich in the mineral wealth from the bowels of
the earth, and as such a rich young man, he should have tempted
many a female heart with his eligible affluence. But nobody
wanted to hold hands with him however, and he was an
unwelcome visitor in Olympus, where the rest of the family
found his profession rather embarrassing, and really wished he
would stop sitting around the place staring at them in his strange
fashion.

Finally Zeus could no longer stand this sexually starved brother of his, who kept eyeing the **Muses** with such a strange gleam in his orbs, so he arranged a marriage for him to **Persephone** the daughter of Demeter.

Neither Persephone nor **Demeter** was consulted in this matter, as Zeus intended killing two birds with one stone in this clever little arrangement. Demeter was becoming increasingly popular with the inhabitants of earth, and as an 'Old Goddess', she was a painful reminder to Zeus (rather like a continual nagging tooth-ache) of his lowly and quite recent beginings, before his rise to power as Chief God. Therefore he decided to depress her psychologically (in case she ever had ideas of toppling him from his newly gained throne in Olympus) by having her daughter stolen from her.

Persephone the symbol of Spring, was simply abducted one day, and taken to live in the gloomy, cold, under-ground palace of Pluto, where absolutely *no one had ever heard of central-heating!*

A family feud broke out in Olympus over this abduction, Demeter went on Strike; and a famine overtook the earth; but Zeus would not allow Persephone to leave the Underworld, no matter what tactics Demeter used in order to force him. He did however eventually agree to allow Persephone to return home to her mother for one part of the year, as she found her husband far too depressing to remain with for more than four months at a time.

After his marriage, Pluto didn't turn up in Olympus so often, and the Gods breathed a collective sigh of relief – happy to be rid of the grinning face of death, and to be free from the smell of embalming fluid in their salon!

Pallas Athena

One might truthfully describe Athena as a *'Daddy's Girl'!*

This description would not only be true figuratively but also literally, because Athena is reputed to have sprung from Zeus' head, *without any help from Hera at all!*

According to the myth, one fine day, Athena emerged fully grown (and in battle dress) from the head of Zeus, and as his special brain-child, proved to be a great source of consolation to him in all his tribulations in affairs of State.

She was a **Virgin Goddess of Civilization,** and a very Militant Goddess of Education and Science. Athena sincerely believed that all education and civilization were best implanted at the tip of a sword, and the idea of 'sparing the rod and spoiling the child' never crossed her mind at all!

She was a fierce and ruthless battle Goddess, as the **Trojans** found to their grief, and Zeus entrusted her to carry his Thunderbolts for him, which in those times was something akin to giving your daughter a nuclear bomb to carry around in her handbag! As an educationist and scientist, this carrying of armaments was appropriate behaviour for Athena, because both education and science are designed to uphold the power of the State, and scientists are always producing weapons which can be used by the Rulers to destroy the people. (We would never have had to fear the 'Neutron' bomb today, if some scientist hadn't invented the damn thing in the first place, and then given it to the Government!)

In the contest between herself and Poseidon as to the naming of Athens, she is said to have clinched the deal by giving the people the 'olive tree', and thus securing their support. However there are other theories about this also, and some said that possibly there were more women in Athens at that time, and that they influenced the vote, and others thought that as the educated and early scientific population of the city were more powerful and vocal than the sailors, then Athena was therefore chosen over **Poseidon.**

Head of Athena Lemnia: by Pheidias, 440 B.C.

She is often depicted as a flashing-eyed, or steely-grey-eyed virgin of wisdom, with an owl as her bird and sign, and it is difficult to imagine her as the sort of girl a young man might like to take on a date. This is probably why she never had any trouble protecting her virginity! After all, who wants to be seen in a restaurant, with a helmetted female with an owl on her shoulder, and a thunderbolt and spear in her hands (not to mention the shield with which she kept beating her opponents over the head with?)

The **Parthenon** in Athens was her special temple, but she was equally popular everywhere in the Greek world, because people realised that you had to have education in order to improve your standard of living.

Athena

Phoebus Apollo

Apollo was the son of Zeus and a lady-love of his, **Leton (Latona)** and he was born with his twin sister **Artemis** on the island of **Delos.**

He has been called the 'most Greek of all the Gods'. Possibly this is because the other Gods who came before him were really the stolen figments of other people's imaginations as we know

Apollo with *Nymphs*

that Pallas Athena was also worshipped by the **Trojans,** and who knows but even Zeus may have had his roots in Egypt or China!

Certainly Apollo was an industrious God, *in name at least,* because he is called the God of Light, Truth, Arts, and the First Healer! This seems a heavy load for such a young man to carry, but he didn't actually spend much time at work, but rather in the pursuit of pleasure. Like Zeus his father, he had a taste for attacking maidens everywhere.

Head of Apollo

He played on a **Lyre,** which had been made for him by Hermes, and he spent a great deal of time in **Delphi,** where as the God of Truth (or Oracle) he spoke to petitioners and seekers of Wisdom, by sending steam through a crack in the rocks, and this form of gaseous elocution was interpreted by a priestess – *for a suitable sum of money of course!*

With Apollo, medicine began – or a least the recognition of medicine and the Art of Healing. As a child, he had been playing in the caves of Parnassus near Delphi, when a huge python which had been troubling the area, came upon him and prepared to devour this infant God of Light. Apollo laughingly strangled the snake and thereby gave the Medical Profession their symbol of serpents which they use to this day.

Besides killing snakes and telling the Truth, Apollo spent a great deal of his time in the woods – either hunting animals with his twin sister – or hunting young maidens by himself!

There is an interesting story concerning him with the maiden **Daphne, or Laurel,** as she is sometimes known.

Daphne/Laurel, was a very liberated girl, who liked running around the forests, eluding sexually rapacious young men. The daughter of **Peneus,** the **River God,** Daphne did not want to have either mortal or immortal lovers as she had no desire to ruin her figure by giving birth to seven children, and to then die of boredom as an Athenian housewife! Similarly she had no desire to be raped by a God, and have to journey to some desolate island, in order to bear her illegitimate child in lonely disgrace.

Being a very determined young woman as well as completely frigid, she managed to fill her time in hunting happily and safely, until one day when the God of Art espied her, and took to the chase.

As Apollo was gaining on her, Daphne cried aloud to her father to save her, and the best thing Peneus could come up with on such short notice was to change her into a Daphne or Laurel tree – just as Apollo's arms were embracing her. From that time on, the Laurel tree was always associated with Apollo as he kept running around the forests kicking out at the tree trunks in sexual frustration.

Another unfortunate love affair which Apollo had, was with the mortal **Coronis,** who lived in Thessaly. The adjective 'unfortunate' naturally applies to the girl – not Apollo!

Coronis was a very a very beautiful maiden (not lacking in confidence) who liked to play the field, and who had many admirers – both mortal and immortal. Apollo of course wanted to be the *ONLY ONE*! and consequently he kept spying on her in order to make sure of this. News regarding her infidelity was brought back to him one day by way of his pet crow (who at that stage in time was a white bird) and the God of Light and Truth became so furious to hear that his emotions were unrequited (not for the first time either!) that he turned the poor bird black, and then killed Coronis and threw her body on a funeral pyre.

As Coronis' body was burning to perdition, Apollo suddenly realised that she was pregnant, and taking the foetus from her sizzling corpse, he placed it inside himself, to keep until it was ready to be born.

It is hoped that the Reader is not gasping with admiration at this feat, because in actual fact it was a very hackneyed old trick. Zeus had done the same thing himself with young **Dionysos** the God of Wine, and Apollo was simply trying to ape his old man!

The baby was then given to a **Centaur** (Horse-man) to bring-up, and he grew to be **Aesculapius,** the mortal who knew all the secrets of medicine, and who helped Mankind with his great skill. Like **Prometheus** the Universal Benefactor, he thought 'thoughts too great for men!' He even developed power over death itself, as he was able to *revive the dead!* Naturally enough Zeus got terrified to see this clever mortal emerge on the scene, so he slew him and sent him down to Hades. But back on earth, Aesculapius had already become the patron of the ill and suffering, and was secretly worshipped by many who found it cheaper (and sometimes more satisfactory) to pray for good health, rather than to visit a doctor.

Apollo was a trifle disconcerted about what had happened to his son, but after Zeus had punished him also (for mental insubordination) he began to see the wisdom of the action, and accepted the decisions of the Captain of the Gods.

The moral of this story is that people must stop trying to over-reach themselves, as they are only tempting the fury of the Gods. 'Know Thyself' the Ancient Greek motto meant to accept your station in life, and never to try to 'buck the System' by endeavouring to prove your superiority to those in charge. In other words if you're poor and starving, and lower class to boot, just resign yourself to your situation – because the Gods are never going to let you get up!

Artemis

Artemis, the twin sister of **Apollo,** was the Patroness of all Wild Things. She was also Huntswoman in Chief to the Gods (whatever that may mean, as being pure spirits, the Gods *weren't supposed to be indulging in real meat!*) but she seemed to spend most of her time killing old and weak animals and protecting the young. She also used her silver arrows to bring a swift and painless death to women who were in great suffering, so she could really be called the Goddess of Euthanasia.

As Apollo was often called the Sun God (especially in Delos where the twins had been born) so Artemis was often referred to as the Moon Goddess. The mother of the twins had been abandoned by Zeus when he discovered she was pregnant, and had wandered unhappily around the Mediterranean for some time until finally the island of Delos gave her hospitality and a chance to bring up her heavenly children.

Being the daughter of a 'fallen woman' seemed to have affected Artemis very strongly because she was a Man-Hater of the first degree; scorned all members of the Male Sex; and put under her protection all girls who wished to avoid masculine attention.

She was hardly ever to be found in Olympus as she despised all banquets and such like foolery, preferring the company of animals to people; and spent most of her time alone in the forests, only occasionally coming back to Olympus for a change of clothing.

She sided with her brother Apollo in all matter of politics, as she couldn't be bothered taking a more personal and active interest in the affairs of any creatures – other than animals. As far as Artemis was concerned, Human Beings were lower than dogs, and there are probably a great many people who would agree with her on this point!

There might even be said to have been some type of genetic or sex mix-up in the case of Artemis and Apollo, because Apollo

Artemis

followed the more feminine line (in all senses of the word) while Artemis followed the masculine. Of course psychologists might lay the blame for this strange attitude of Artemis' on her early childhood in Delos when she grew up without any male parent to relate to. But whatever the reason, Artemis definitely didn't like men, and spent as little time as possible with them. Virginity for Artemis was more than just a passing whim or fancy. It was a way of Life!

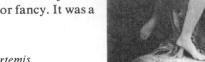

Artemis

Aphrodite

The Goddess of Love and Beauty, Aphrodite, was another illegitimate child of Zeus, whose mother (according to rumour) had been **Dione,** and Aphrodite had been born from the sea foam near **Cythera,** and then wafted off to **Cyprus,** to bide her time until she was big enough to stand on her own against Hera in Olympus.

Aphrodite and *Eros*

Aphrodite teaching *Eros* how to shoot.
Aphrodite and *Pan*

57

Aphrodite playing with Erotes

Hera absolutely loathed this Goddess of Love, who spent her time in constantly painting her face, washing her hair, and primping herself in continual preparation for romance. Between these two Goddesses there was a perpetual feud, and **Olympus** was never exactly a 'happy home' with the two of them there together.

In order to remove this 'sex-crazy wanton' from the scene, Hera attempted to arrange a marriage between her and **Hephaestus** the laim and ugly God of the Forge. But this

The *"Capitoline Aphrodite"* 320 B.C., Roman copy

Aphrodite of Knidos: by Praxiteles, 350 B.C.

marriage of convenience didn't stop Aphrodite from enjoying herself with other suitors, and her wings remained unclipped.

Aphrodite lived entirely for love (after all that was her profession) and when she didn't receive attention, she became sulky and morose, and took to studying her face in the bathroom mirror for hours on end, wondering if she had developed any lines in that perfect oval.

The *Venus de Milo*

Venus and Area: by Rubens

Whenever a 'new beauty' was discovered on earth, Aphrodite would descend to take a look, and if she felt the slightest bit threatened, would rid herself of her competitor by arranging a skilful bit of metamorphosis, so that the unfortunate girl might suddenly find herself changed into a star, or a flower, or even a bird!

She had a son, **Eros,** who was obviously born out of wed-lock, but as the Olympians were exceedingly hypocritical on points of morality (certain points anyway!) they pretended that this small cherub was merely a companion, or baby brother of Aphrodites'. She was not in fact a very attentive mother, but used sometimes to take Eros with her on her trips to earth, so that he could shoot his 'love arrows' into the hearts of mortals, over whom she wished to cast a spell.

Aphrodite's temples in ancient Athens were an early form of 'Brothel', where the 'Customers' came and worshipped by honouring the priestesses with their attentions and then paid them in the form of a donation to the temple. On special feast days the queues outside the temples stretched for miles, and the wealth of the temples increased accordingly. State run prostitution was an extremely lucrative business then – as it is today!

Venus Anadyomene: by Ingres

Hermes

Hermes the God of Commerce, was also the special **Messenger of the Gods,** and notorious for bringing bad messages at that!

In addition to his main occupations in commerce and communications, he was the special 'side kick' of Zeus, and spent much of his time arranging meetings (you know what kind of meetings Zeus was having!) hushing up scandals, and putting the 'strong arm' on anyone who had a difference of opinion with his boss.

Zeus was the father of this Patron Saint of Merchants and he was conceived by **Maia,** the daughter of **Atlas,** who having served her purpose in pleasuring Zeus, and in giving birth to Hermes, disappears from the mythology completely. But then c'est la vie! – especially for women!

Hermes always wore special sandals made of gold, which meant that he could speed around the place doing *more bad things* in a *shorter time* than anyone else! He also wore a type of crowned hat (which showed his superiority to other un-hatted Gods) and that is probably why business men and executives of today also feel they have to doñ some form of head-gear, in order to prove that they are men of affluence and power! This affection for hats is definitely an interesting psychological aspect of the human character, but the Author thinks that possibly she won't pursue the subject further, but will continue with the Greek myths, as she set out to do, and therefore the Reader need not become anxious.

From the very first day that he was born, Hermes was up to no good! On that initial day of life, he stole the herds of Apollo, and made the God of Arts extremely angry, as even artists need to have some sort of property investments in order to tide them over 'resting' periods, and cows are as good a form of investment as anything else.

Zeus made Hermes give them back – which he finally did (after having discovered that he couldn't sell them anywhere else, in

Mercury giving the golden Apple of the garden of the Hesperides to
Paris: by Annibale Caracci

order to make a profit on the beef market) and to prove his repentance, and re-instate himself in the good graces of Apollo again, he made him a present of the world's first 'lyre', which he had just invented. So, music came into the world for the first time.

In order to earn extra pocket money for himself, Hermes worked down in Hades for his uncle Pluto, taking customers to the funeral parlour. During times of great upheaval, like the **Trojan War,** he amassed a fortune from this activity, as the dead *all had to pay to enter* **Hades!** – and Hermes was always the first to get his ten percent!

All the Greeks worshipped him as a shrewd and cunning thief, and there were altars to him in all the markets, and along the roads, and throughout the city centres and main areas of commerce.

Hermes was also said to be the father of **Pan** and **Silenus,** and if this is true, then it is most surprising. Both these characters were much more honest than their father, and neither followed his footsteps in commerce, but took to drink and whoring instead. However, it is mysterious but true nevertheless, that whereas a drunk, or a libertine, generally hurts no one but himself, and *never exploits others* – a merchant is always much more highly thought of! So most of the Greeks were of the opinion that Pan and Silenus were a disgrace to their clever father, and should have been horse whipped for being such loose – living and shiftless hobos.

No matter what some people like to say – *MONEY IS EVERYTHING! That is why Hermes was so popular with all the ancient Greeks and Romans!*

Ares

Ares the God of War, was the son of Zeus and Hera, and equally detested by both parents, who each naturally blamed the other for all the faults which they saw in him.

The main problem with Ares was that he was a *COWARD* – and a very noisy coward into the bargain! He was always howling around the place with a full company of horrors, such as **Eris,** his sister (also known as **Discord**) **Strife,** her son, and the Goddess of War, **Enyo** (Bellona in Latin) plus the trio, Terror, Trembling, and Panic.

Nobody in Olympus could stand any of them because of the abominable sounds they made. It was a bit like having a pop group practising in the house continually, and when they weren't locked up in Ares' room, rehearsing battle cries and moans, then they were in and out of everyone's way, and picking quarrels the whole time!

Sometimes Ares went down to earth when there was a battle going on, and would walk around the fields, moaning and screaming, and generally carrying on. But whenever the going got rough, then he'd always leave rapidly, and head back to Olympus for a glass of milk and a nap.

Most of the time, the soldiers told him to get out of their way, because they felt they could better devote themselves to the job of killing each other, without having to contend with the problem of Ares' obstructionist presence.

He was supposedly born in **Thrace,** because reputedly that's where the rudest Greeks lived, but some people say they have found them to be just as rude in Athens and Salonica – not to mention Hydra!

The 'dog' was one of his symbols, which was very unjust, because dogs are not aggressive by nature, and only fight because people push them too. The 'vulture' was his other symbol, and seems to be appropriate enough.

Hephaestus and Thetis

Ares was madly in love with Aphrodite, and wherever she went, so did he, consequently Love and War became generally fused together in the Greek mind. There were also some rumours that Aphrodite actually married him, but others said that really she was just having as affair with him on the side, like the many others which she enjoyed whenever it was expedient for her.

Not worshipped in Greek cities over much (at least not openly, as the Greeks liked to think of themselves as a peaceful people!) Ares only really came into his own when he emigrated to Rome, and found as so many migrants do, that new places present new opportunities!

Hephaestus/Vulcan/Mulciber

Hephaestus was the God of Fire, or the Forge, and as the son of Zeus and Hera, there are many stories concerning him.

One account says that **Zeus** was not really sure that Hephaestus actually came from his loins as they say, and because he thought that Hera had been offering herself around, he took the baby and threw him out of Olympus, in order to save his face (and cut down on the food bills at the same time!)

There is yet another story that Hephaestus was not made lame and maimed by Zeus throwing him around, but that he was *born that way,* and that Hera took a dislike to him because he was so ill-formed, so *she threw him* out of Olympus, and maimed him *even more* than he already was! (Both stories depict early 'baby-bashing' in Olympus – Social Workers Please Note!)

Whatever the truth of the matter is, Hephaestus was the only God not perfect, and beside his body being a little screwed up, his mind must also have been rather slow, therefore the family of Beauty, Order, and Justice were a little confused on what to do with him. It could be said that Hephaestus was ruining the Olympian Perfection Image slightly!

Finally the family hit on the solution of keeping him in a workshop at the back of the house, and they only let him into the front parlour on *very special occasions* (like the time he was married to **Aphrodite** in order to provide her with a legitimate father for **Eros!**)

He was quite happy however, puttering around in his workshop, as he was keen on working with his hands, and he made all sorts of things, including some moving golden statues which helped him in his craftwork.

As Hephaestus showed such talent, Zeus decided to make him the Patron and Protector of all the Smiths of Greece, and he was very popular in Athens; especially with the children of the city, who were very impressed with the idea of his having golden mechanical, female robots.

"A God for Everyone, and Everyone for a God!" The Olympian Motto

In fact Hephaestus fulfilled the need for a God for all the *Idiots of Greece,* and for the *Workers* in the *Sweat-Shops* of the various City States, and thus the System was able to use him – even though he wasn't perfect like the other Olympian Deities.

Hestia

Hestia was the typical 'old maid' of Olympus, who did all the work, and received none of the thanks – because it is the Marys of this world who always get all the attention, and not the Marthas!

Poor Hestia was another of Zeus' sisters, and like **Athena** and **Artemis** she was also a virgin. However, in the case of Hestia – nobody thought it a shame!

Without her, no one would ever have had a meal (of ambrosia and nectar) on time, and the place would never have been swept, because as Zeus was always out (picking up women) and Hera always out (chasing after him) it was left to Hestia to see that the fire in the hearth never went out, and that Olympus as the Home and Heart of the System, survived!

As the Goddess of the Hearth she was very important, but in an underhand and unannounced way. All new born children were carried around their family hearths and dedicated to her, and each city and colony of Greece (and later, Rome also) had a continual fire burning which symbolised the 'Home', and Hestia. All meals were begun and ended with a special prayer to her, and she was beseeched to preserve the sanctity of the Family Life and to keep the Home Fires Burning.

Zeus and Hera might have been the aknowledged leaders of Olympus, but it was Hestia who kept the whole place together. When the Gods had gone to Rome (after the fall of the Greeks) Hestia became known as Vesta, and developed into a much more important Deity, with vestal virgins in her temples and all sorts of extra doo-dads.

The Romans very wisely realised the value of a secure family life, and of its influence on the *political life* of a nation, and therefore Vestia, like Ares, thoroughly enjoyed the change of scene, and the new honours heaped on her hardworking head!

Hestia at Work. The true Hearth and Heart of the Whole System.

Hestia

73

CHAPTER III

OTHER DEITIES IN AND OUT OF OLYMPUS
The Lesser Gods of Olympus

Eros, the **God of Love (Cupid,** in Latin) was *either* the son, *or,* the companion of Aphrodite. It is assumed in fact that he was really her 'love child', and a remarkably troublesome one at that!

Eros taking a nap

He was always represented as a small, fat baby, who spent his time walking around Olympus carrying a bow and arrow, and wearing *only* a sash, and a blind-fold. As he was always sprying on people; telling tales; and being a *general pain in the ass;* the adults of Olympus had resorted to tying up his eyes with a cloth, so that he wouldn't be able to see what anyone was doing, and with whom!

Eros had three baby-sitters in attendance on him most of the time. They were **Anteros** – the Avenger of Slighted Love; **Himeros** – Longing; and **Hymen** – the God of the Wedding Feast.

He was an extremely mischievous, in fact, evil child, and was, always throwing his darts in the wrong places, because as it is said, "Love is Blind"; and Eros (due to the material covering his orbs) couldn't see in order to aim properly. But even if he *had* been able to take his blind-fold off, he would still have thrown his arrows in the wrong places – because that was the type of child he was!

Hebe was the **Goddess of Youth,** and the daughter of Zeus and Hera. Apart from being young, she was a rather dull person who did nothing to merit a mention in mythology, besides marrying Hercules the strongest man in the world. The marriage didn't work out (due to Hercules' terrible temper) and Hebe faded, with her youth, into the mists of time.

Iris was the **Goddess of the Rainbow,** and another messenger of the Gods. She was definitely colourful – but not much else!

Graces. These were three beautiful sisters who were forever laughing and giggling around the place, and driving Hera mad with their chatter.

Cupid making a bow out of the club of *Hercules*

75

Three Muses: by Praxiteles

They were: **Aglaia** – Splendour; **Euphrosyne** – Mirth; and **Thalia** – Good Cheer.

This lithesome trio were always dancing around the house in time to Apollo's lyre, and singing and laughing fit to bust a gut! No dinner party in Olympus was complete without them, but Hera somehow just couldn't seem to appreciate how dreary the place would be if they weren't there. It is strange but true, that sour unhappy people never seem to take pleasure in the happiness of others more cheerful and optimistic.

The Muses: These were nine beautiful and intelligent young ladies, who wandered the halls and gardens of Olympus instilling culture and education into everyone who happened to be unfortunate enough to caught by them.

They were very bohemian, and had strange ideas on fashion and hair-colour, which they felt should be in lilac tones, so they

The Three *Graces*

were known as the "Violet Tressed Lovelies" of Olympus.

The Muses accompanied Apollo everywhere, and sang and danced and told stories and educated each others' minds – and never let anyone watch television because it was so bad for their mental development!

There was **Clio** for History, **Urania** for Astronomy, **Melpomene** for Tragedy, **Thalia** for Comedy, **Terspichore** for Dance, **Calliope** for Epic Poetry, **Erato** for Love Poetry, **Polyhymnia** for Songs of the Gods, and **Euterpe** for Lyric Poetry.

This lot made Hera feel distinctly illiterate, and Athena –

77

distinctly jealous! Aphrodite simply couldn't stand the colour of their hair, and Zeus was positively intimidated! But they had to stay whether the Olympians liked it or not, because when you are rich and influential, then you've got to look the part, and it's absolutely essential to have a bit of culture in the home. It's the same reasoning behind most of the modern twentieth century 'gentry' buying oil paintings, and subscribing to concerts and plays which bore them flat. People with money have to develop good taste, *whether they like it or not!* And so Zeus and his family (who were really rather vulgar and sloppy, and not as 'blue-blooded' as they liked to pretend) felt that the Muses had to be trotted out and shown to guests in order to impress them with the high degree of civilization of the house-hold.

The best of the Muses was naturally Thalia, however even she got too much on occasions, and took to playing practical jokes on people, and becoming hysterical at her own witticisms. But then all humourists do this from time to time, as creating comedy is a sad and lonely business, and sometimes only the comedian himself can fully appreciate how funny a situation is.

Besides the above spirits running around Olympus, Zeus also had two 'Gentleman's Gentlemen'. One was called Themis, which means 'Right' or 'Divine Justice', and the other was 'Dike' which means 'Human Justice'. In addition to these two austere personages, there were also two secretaries, **'Nemesis'** (Righteous Anger) and **'Aidos'** (Reverence, or Shame). These last two employees did not live-in, but only came to clear up some office work and left again each evening as Hera said that she had quite enough to contend with, without having them continually under her feet.

There was also Eris, the evil Goddess of Discord and friend of Ares, but she was not a frequent visitor to Olympus, because she always created a row of some kind, and whenever they saw her coming up the path, the Olympians closed the doors and drew the blinds, and pretended that everyone had gone to Earth for the day.

Nemesis

The Gods of the Waters

Poseidon, or Neptune (as he was known to the Romans) was the most important watery God. He was the Lord and Ruler of the 'Sea' i.e. the Mediterranean, and the 'Friendly Sea', i.e. the **Euxine** or **Black Sea.** He also controlled all the underground rivers as well, and was inclined to argue with his brother Pluto over the sovreignty of the waters of the Underworld.

Besides Poseidon there were some other liquid deities, for example, **Ocean** a Titan who was the Lord of the **River Ocean,** which was the great river encircling the earth. His wife who was also a Titan, was called **Tethys,** and the **Oceanids** were the nymphs or daughters of Ocean and Tethys.

The sons of this marriage were all the rivers on the earth itself, but sometimes they changed sex and became female rivers in order to be difficult, or because different people had different ideas about how the mythology should read. Actually by the time the Gods left for Rome, there were as many different versions of Mythology then as there are of the 'Holy Bible' today, and naturally everyone said that *their version was the correct one!*

There was also **Pontus,** the 'Deep Sea', who was a son of Mother Earth, and as he was the father of **Nereus,** was a very important sea god.

Nereus was called the **'Old Man of the Sea'** long before Hemingway wrote a book with this name, and he was a trusty, good, and gentle god, whose wife was **Doris,** the daughter of Ocean. These two gave birth to fifty lovely daughters, who were the **Nereids** or nymphs of the Ocean, and **Thetis,** who was one of the fifty, was the mother of **Achilles** of Trojan fame. Poseidon himself married another, called **Amphitrite,** but this didn't prevent him from running around with a lot of mermaids as well.

Triton was the trumpeter of the Sea, and kept blowing on a large shell, and stirring things up all the time. He was the son of Poseidon and Amphitrite.

The Mildenhall Dish

Nereid sarcophagus

There seems to have been some doubts concerning the origins of **Proteus,** a deity who could change shape and foretell the future. Some said that he was Poseidon's attendant, and others, that he was his illegitimate son by some foreign nymph or other. Poseidon led such a loose and lusty life that it would be impossible to know for sure about a thing like this, and probably even Poseidon didn't know himself.

Then there were the **Naiads,** the water nymphs, who dwelt in brooks and springs and fountains, and hung around trying to pick up and 'do over' any unfortunate males who happened to fall into their clutches. The Naiads were more dangerous than New York 'muggers' (and twice as numerous) and were to be avoided at all costs!

Nereid sarcophagus

The Underworld

The chief God of the Underworld was called Hades, or Pluto, or **Dis.** It didn't really matter one called him, the main point was to avoid him as long as possible! Most Greeks just referred to him by pointing their fingers in a downward movement towards the earth, and refrained from ever using his name in case he should decide to come up for a visit!

Hell itself was also known as Hades, and the entrance to the place was across the Ocean, beneath the earth, and by way of some caverns and deep lakes.

There were two divisions of Hades. **Erebus** was the area where the dead first passed as soon as they had expired, and then there was **Tartarus,** the deeper region, and prison itself.

Persephone was the unwilling queen of this dominion, and she lived in the palace of Pluto, which was richly decorated and crowded with innumerable guests – especially in times of war and famine.

Outside the castle there were wastelands, wan and cold, with strange ghosty flowers, and as the Headquarters of the King of Death were so badly constructed, Pluto had to spend a fortune on heating in order to try and keep Persephone warm.

There were a great many rivers running through this region and they were as follows: **Acheron,** the river of Woe; **Cocytus,** the river of Lamentation; **Phlegethon,** the river of Fire; **Styx,** the river of Unbreakable Oaths; and **Lethe,** the river of Forgetfulness. (N.B. It is not recorded whether there were any fish in any of them, so the fanatic angler should not go tearing off to his death without first checking into the matter thoroughly!)

Charon, an aged boatman, ferried the souls of the dead across the water to the gates of Tartarus, and being a keen business man, would only ferry the souls of people on whose lips some passage money had been placed. Death is a costly business like everything else, and if a soul didn't have the fare for the boat trip, then he had to stay on the further bank and spend his eternity

watching other people going in to a party at Pluto's place, and wishing that he could go back up into the world and get killed all over again; in order to come down with his entrance money at the ready and buy a boat ticket. But dying is like being born – you only get the chance to do it once, and if you mess it up, then you never get another opportunity to put it right!

Outside the gates of Tartarus, sat **Cerberus,** the threeheaded, and dragon-tailed dog (who would never have won any prize at all in Cruft's Dog Show) and he made sure that everybody went before the three Judges, **Rhadamanthus, Minos,** and **Aeacus;** who sentenced people to everlasting dammation if they had been bad, or to everlasting joy in the Elysian Fields, if they had been good.

The **Elysian Fields** were supposed to be a really charming place from what one reads of them, but the Ancient Greeks were as sceptical as a group of Package Tourists, and knew that no matter what was written about the place as an attractive resort, *they wouldn't like it, and that they wouldn't get their money's worth!*

Nobody in Ancient Greece was really enthusiastic about dying, no matter how blameless a life he or she had led! We may therefore assume that in the Elysian Fields, the plumbing didn't work, the food was inferior (and generally cold) and that the lifts kept breaking down. Unfortunately for everyone, Pluto was always more concerned with his matrimonial problems than with improving his business and making death easier and more enjoyable for his clientele.

Hades was popular though with the **Erinyes,** who used not only to holiday there often, but also regarded it as a second home, and as a place of absolute relaxation from their normal monotonous routine of pursuing the mortals on earth for their various misdemeanours, and then revenging them in diverse ghastly ways.

Sleep and his brother **Death** also dwelt in the Lower World, and carried on a type of Cottage Industry from there. They sent up dreams to people, which ascended through two gates. The

Caeretan Hydria depicting Hercules, delivering the hound of Hades, *Cerverus,* to his master Eurystheus

one gate of horn, was for true dreams, and the other of ivory, was for false.

The modern reader of mythology is indebted to **Virgil** for this geographic account, because Virgil (a typically industrious and poetically romantic Celt in the Roman Empire) really got to grips with the problems of the Underworld, and spent a lot of time describing the place. The Greeks themselves preferred to leave the lower regions to the imagination, as they never welcomed the thought of death. But the **Roman Civilization** was much more sensible and pragmatic about the whole thing and wanted detailed maps from their Celtic explorers so that they could build roads and aqueducts.

Truly it can be said that the British are the heirs to the Roman Empire because they are just as practical a people, and would be constructing Public Toilets, and Telephone Boxes all over Hades, if given the chance. And naturally, the first question the average Briton would ask you about the Underworld nowadays, is whether the cigarettes are taxed, and how much Duty Free is allowed?

The Lesser Gods of Earth

The Earth herself was called the 'All-mother of the World', but she was not really a divinity, and not personified and separated from the actual earth itself – at least not after Zeus had established his Captaincy!

Demeter and **Dionysos** were the supreme deities of earth, and after them came Pan, who was Hermes' son, and he was a noisy, merry, zoomorphic being with a goat's horns and hooves, and a God's taste for young nymphs!

Pan was born in **Arcady,** the rustic idyll made famous by Virgil, and he was the Goatherd's God, and the Shepherd's God, plus the God of all the Drunks!

He loved nature and wild places, and played on special reed pipes to serenade his current amours. Always rejected in love, he took out his sexual frustration by wild and rowdy behaviour at night and mid-day, and spread terror in the breasts of travellers by the sounds he made. It is because of this idiosyncrasy of his that the word 'Panic' developed from his name. He was never terribly popular with the City Greeks who considered him a rough, uncouth villager.

Silenus, was said by some, to be the son of Pan; and by others, to be the son of Hermes. It is a little difficult to think of him as the son of either, because he was always considerably older than both of them!

Silenus was a jovial, fat, old man, who rode an ass because he was always too drunk to be able to walk, and he was often in the company of Dionysos, as well as Pan. He is supposed to have been the tutor of Dionysos when the God of Wine was young, but in this instant, the pupil became the teacher, and *taught his master to be a drunk!* **Silenus** never recovered from the experience of teaching Dionysos, and to the end of his days, slopped around the countryside, pouring alcohol down his throat as if Prohibition were just around the corner! (Quite possibly this drinking had nothing whatsoever to do with Dionysos as such, but was simply the result of the whole painful teaching experience. The author has had some experience with teaching, herself, and feels that, this profession is more inclined to drive people to alcoholism than any other!)

Besides these disreputable drunken deities there were the Heavenly Twins, **Castor** and **Pollux,** who spent their time up in Heaven and down on Earth – equally; and who were used as stars by the sailors at night. They were the sons of Leda, the woman who liked running around with swans, and their father was either King **Tyndareus of Sparta,** or Zeus of Olympus. As the boys were only half immortal, it is left to the Reader to try and work out for himself exactly who sired them; but regardless of their pedigree they led a pretty busy life before they took to the skies, including an extremely complicated bore hunt in Calydonia, the original name for Scotland.

Castor got stabbed in some dispute over women and had to go to Hades because his immortality wasn't 100%, and Pollux decided to stay with him and keep him company as a form of solidarity. So they shared their life and death, with each other, and took turns in being alive and dead, which confused everyone everywhere, and the Gods got so tired of the whole affair that they put them to work in the sky; as stars to aid all ships in distress.

The Sileni were zoomorphic creatures, part man, and part horse, but they walked on two legs, not on four, and had horses' hooves, ears, and tails. The only thing they ever seem to have done was to pose for ancient Greek vases, on which they can still be seen. Apart from their cultural contribution to pottery there is nothing much in mythology about them. Doubtless they were meant to show the transitional development of the 'Homo

A limp *Dionysos*, holding a lyre is supported by Ariadne, while Eros plays for them.

Sapien' from Animal to Man, as the Greeks were aware of the Evolutionary Theory long before Darwin found out about it!

The Satyrs, like Pan, were goat-men, and lived in wild places, and followed Dionysos around like a band of early hippies or gypsies, or bored and lonely unemployed. Possibly they were down-and-out alcoholics who were looking for a free drink, but perhaps they shouldn't be dismissed so disparagingly because they proved to be the inspiration for the birth of Drama and Tragedy in Greece.

The Nymphs were called **Oreads** in the mountains, and Dryads in the trees, and were beautiful, sexy, loose-living women, just hanging around to drag down and morally degrade those good-living, pure, country-boy, wholesome Greek Men!

There were also Centaurs, who were half men and half horse, and these were all savage creatures, apart from Chiron, the Centaur who gave his life in place of Prometheus in later versions of mythology. Also, the Centaur who taught Apollo's son medicine and brought him up, was likewise noble and cultivated, but the rest, according to the Greeks were sheer rubbish!

Then there were the **Gorgons,** who were dragon-like creatures who turned men to stone (just by looking at them) and the Graiae were extra-special Gorgons who lived on the far bank of Ocean and had one telescopic eye between them.

Most Ancient Greeks felt it their duty to run out and try cutting off a Gorgon head or two before their twenty-first birthday, as a sort of Puberty Ritual. However, the Gorgons were a pretty solid breed and no matter how many heads they lost, they kept on growing new ones, and delighted in giving the mortals something to do with themselves on hot summer evenings in the Mediterranean area.

The Sirens lived on an island in what was called the 'Sea', but which was really the Mediterranean Sea. The Greeks were so ignorant that they thought it was the only sea in the world (or the only one worth bothering about) and that's why they didn't know the right name to call it (unlike we knowledgeable people of to-day!)

These Sirens had enchanting voices, but no one had any idea what they looked like, because no one who had ever seen them had ever returned! But it's certain that they looked better than the police car sirens which we have today. They must have sounded better to, or else nobody would ever have bothered to have written about them.

The Fates or **Moirae,** were three women who gave good or evil forecasts to people at their birth, and who were the original design for the 'Fairy Godmother' of northern European stories.

They were **Clotho,** *the Spinner of the Thread of Life;* **Lachesis,** the Disposer of Lots, who assigned Destiny; and **Atropos,** who Could Not Be Turned, and who carried around a 'Shear' to *cut off the Thread of Life!* She (Atropos) was the really dangerous one, and was always walking around and getting entangled with her two sisters, and due to her shortsightedness, cutting off the wrong thread before its time!

These three old maids were always gossiping, and fighting together, and disposing of everybody's fate the wrong way, and Clotho would no sooner get started on spinning someone a 'Life Thread', than Atropos would cut the damned thing off! Even Zeus kept away from these three, because as he said, "You can never be sure!" And Pluto said that they were selfish old cows because they *never* checked with him on how full he was downstairs, but just kept sending him bodies by the dozen whenever they were having a row.

Aeolus was the **King of the Winds** on the island **Aeolia,** and Regent or Vice-Roy to the Gods. There were four chief winds: **Boreas** of the North; **Zephyr,** of the West; **Notus,** of the South; and **Eurus,** the East Wind.

This lot do nothing but blow in and out of mythology a lot, and they never say very much, so the student of mythology should not even bother to try remembering their names.

The *Tower of the Winds* in Athens, an octagonal structure containing a water-clock (mid-1st century B.C.). Each of the eight faces was decorated with a sculptured personification of one of the eight winds.

The Author in fact, wouldn't have bothered to even put them down on this page, except that the Publisher said that the book should be larger, and consequently would have to be padded out a little. Due to this strange attitude on the Publisher's part, the Reader must expect a lot more useless, unrelated, and miscellaneous information from now on. It seems that Quantity and not Quality is what counts in this world nowadays!

The *Winds* (detail from Birth of Venus): by Botticelli

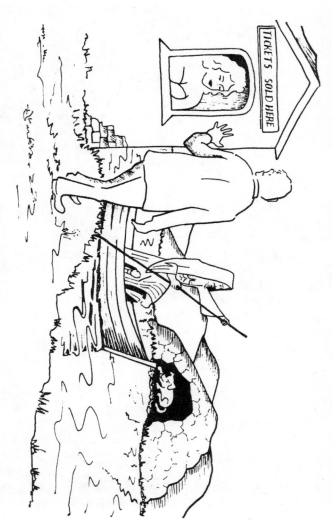

"From Here to Eternity."

CHAPTER IV

THE ROMAN GODS

The Roman Gods were in fact the Greek Gods; but before the Romans stole them, they did have a few of their own; but very boring and nondescript beings who weren't really exciting enough on which to base a complicated State Religion.

Their Gods were generally practical, useful deities, connected with the agricultural background of the Romans, because before they ever had an empire, the Romans were simply small farmers – and very earthy and small-minded, small farmers at that!

The **Numina** were numerous in number and occupation, but lacking in glamour, and were practical spirits who did practical things like rocking baby cradles, and presiding over childrens' food. Two of them however, **'Lares'** and **'Penates'**, were very important in the home.

Lar was the spirit of the store-house, and watched over the family food supply (an awesome undertaking in times of want!) and Penates was the God of the Hearth, and was always worshipped at home and never in a temple. (A type of Neanderthal Hestia!)

Terminus was the God of Boundaries; **Priapus,** the Cause of Fertility; **Pales,** the Strengthener of Cattle; and **Sylvanus,** the Helper of Plowmen. And all these Gods existed and went about their work right next to the family farm-house, because the original Romans didn't have any cities at all!

Saturn was originally one of the Numina and the Protector of the Sowers of the Seed, and his wife, **Ops,** was the Harvest Helper. Later it was said that Saturn was really the Old Greek God **Cronus,** and therefore the father of Zeus or Jupiter (the Romans were dead keen on tracing their ancestry, and establishing their right to world leadership) and Saturnalia was a festival held in December, which later still became our Christmas.

This winter festival was held in Italy to commemorate the Golden Age when Saturn ruled the world, and during this time (in honour of the peace of Saturn) no wars were declared, and slaves and masters ate at the same table, in order to prove how Democratic they all were. Also, executions were postponed – *NOT CANCELLED — ONLY POSTPONED!* And people gave each other presents, and ran around smiling at each other for a few days before they recommenced kicking each other around and killing each other off as usual. (This same hypocritical tradition has been continued by the Christian World in the Twentieth Century, and is the basis for most other religious festivals in every country, as people like nothing better than a little sentimental rest between bouts in the jungle fight for Survival!)

There was another member of the Numina called **Janus,** and he was the **God of Good Beginnings,** and comes down to us in the month of January, and thereby starts our year.

Janus was extremely popular, and feared by the Romans, amd had a big temple in the City, which ran from east to west.

The idea of the two directions was to symbolize the day beginning and the day ending, and there were two doors also, between which stood his statue with two faces – one young, and the other old.

The doors of his temple were only closed closed when Rome was at peace and not at war, and to give you an idea of the character of the Romans it is interesting to note that these doors were only closed three times in the first seven hundred years of Rome's life as a City and Empire!

The first occasion was when Rome was ruled by the good King Numa – or at least according to the Romans he was good! The second time was when the first Punic War had finished and Carthage had been destroyed in 241 B.C.

The third time was in the reign of Augustus, when the Romans had destroyed practically everybody else around the place, and as there was nobody left to fight, the 'Roman Pax' dominated the world!

Besides the above, there was also **Faunus,** who was the grandson of Saturn, and a Roman version of Pan. A type of rustic god and a prophet, he usually spoke in dreams which he sent to men after they had indulged a little too generously in the vino, and then began looking for the veritas! Faunus was usually accompanied by the Fauns, who were **Roman Satyrs.**

The Spirits of the Good Dead in Hades, were called **Manes,** and were worshipped as divine, as the Romans respected their dead ancestors much more than the Greeks, and were extremely fearful and obsequious towards the **Lemure** or **Larvae,** who were the Evil Dead. (Due to the aggressive character of the Romans as Empire Builders, there were always more Lemure around the place than there were Manes!)

Most of the other Roman spirits were very practical types who worked for a living (unlike the Olympians, who really never did anything constructive at all!) As we see, in the primitive Roman homes (before the people became wealthy and sophisticated City-dwellers) the deities were not unlike sheep dogs, who guarded the property and looked after the livestock and inhabitants of the farm, and like sheep-dogs, their individual personalities were not considered to be matters of interest, as only their work made them important!

The **Camenae** were Goddesses such as these, who guarded the wells and cured disease, but when the Greeks arrived in Rome, these down to earth women were converted into personalities akin to the Greek Muses, who cared for impractical abstracts like art and science.

Most of the other common or garden deities of Rome, went-under, in the culture shock of the arrival of the Greek Gods, and as the Romans hastened to change the names of the Olympians to good Latin ones, the original Latin spirits faded away. Anyway, how on earth could they compete with the glamour of Zeus and his family?

The Romans – like most Aristocrats and Imperialists – had their 'Roots' in the Cow-Shed.

CHAPTER V

THE CREATION OF THE WORLD

Unlike all the other stories of Creation which flourish among the peoples of the world, the Ancient Greeks believed that the World Itself, *MADE THE GODS* — and Not, The Gods, *THE WORLD!*

In this respect they are remarkably mentally akin to today's modern scientists, and it follows therefore that should any of them happen to arise from wherever they slumber in the mists of time, they would be able to understand the 'Big Bang' theory, better than the rest of us.

The World, according to the Ancient Greeks, was born from NOTHING.

At first there was only chaos or complete confusion, and from this confused, chaotic nothingness came two children – Night, and **Erebus,** or, Death.

Night and **Death,** finally got together, and managed to bring forth **Love.** (There is really *heavy symbolism* here, if you think about it deeply enough!) Then Love (without the help of anyone) managed to create **Light,** and its companion, **Day.**

All through Greek Mythology there are references to Asexual Reproduction, so the serious reader should not waste his or her time in petty questioning about who the Father was, or where the Mother was, because to the Ancient Greek mind it seems that they didn't need "Two, to Tango!"

Now that Light and Day were in the world and things were moving along in this fairly optimistic fashion, a very solid Mother Earth rose up, accompanied by a rather vague absentee Father Heaven character who doesn't figure very much in things at the start. (This is actually rather true of life in general, and shows the nature of the Male Sex, for after all it is the Mother of the family who does all the really important things like cooking, cleaning, and changing the diapers, while the Father simply drifts in and out of the house attending football games and watching television.)

Doubtless Father Heaven was behaving in this very way while the World was being born and growing-up, but even so he managed to come down to Earth often enough in order to co-produce some monster children as his share in the creation process.

These first off-spring of Earth and Heaven were absolutely diabolical, and not at all the sort of babies one would like to walk around a park and show off, or offer to politicians to chuck under the chin at election time. They were weird and wonderful combinations of dinosaurs and volcanoes and hurricanes and such like.

Three of these monster babies were known as the **Cyclopes,** who by some over-sight in nature possessed only one eye each, but they compensated for this deficiency by the sheer size and grandeur of the only piece of optical equipment which they did have.

Another set of monsters was born waving one hundred hands about, and still another group arrived nodding fifty heads each! (All of these deformed bairns quite possibly mean something symbolic – but nobody seems to have bothered to explain quite what.)

Whatever the symbolism of this period means, Mother Earth kept right on trying to produce something half-way decent (please note the dogged persistence of Womanhood!) and finally came up with the Titans, who, although *also pretty horrible* to behold, at least had pleasant personalities – or some of them had at any rate!

I imagine Mother Earth told them what all mothers tell their children at some time or other, "Looks aren't the only thing that matters in this world. It's better to be beautiful inside, rather than out!"

Whether the Titans really believed this any more than most children do, is debatable, but as they didn't really have anything better looking with which to compare themselves, then they didn't develop Titan-sized inferiority complexes, except for one, named Cronus.

Meanwhile Father Heaven was getting most upset with all these horrible children which his wife kept producing, and naturally, he blamed them all on her. Naturally also, he decided to have them all put away, so he wouldn't have to look at them and be continually reminded of his *own* imperfect genetic structure!

Therefore Heaven locked all the monsters away in the depths of the ground, and left only the Cyclopes and the Titans free to wander at will, through the world.

Now Earth became absolutely furious, as well she might, and turned on Heaven with the aid of her remaining free children. (This was perfectly natural and shows what has always been a typical female reaction through the ages, as Women have *always sided with their sons against their husbands!* Freud probably based his whole understanding of psychology, from a brief browse through Greek Mythology in the Public Library in Vienna one rainy afternoon.)

The Titan Cronus, who was a real 'Mummy's Boy', and who had some sort of complex long before **Oedipus** was invented, decided to 'Do his Daddy in' by a surprise mugging one dark night. But if you can't 'chop your Mamma up in Massachusetts', it's even more difficult to 'chop your Poppa up in Heaven', so he only succeeded in wounding him a little.

Heaven limped off after this encounter, badly gashed, but still alive; and where his blood spattered the ground, there sprang up a race of **Giants.** *Please note that this reproduction is completely without the aid of sexual intercourse with Earth!* But then Heaven probably didn't trust her enough to venture into bed with her anymore – and who can blame him?

Besides these horrible Giants, a group of Furies (Erinyes) was born, who were weird, wild women, with eyes which wept blood copiously, and whose heads were festooned with writhing snakes. (Thanks to that particular evening, these Furies have been around ever since as a form of punishment for all sinners. Four bottles of whisky drunk in rapid succession nowadays generally ensures one the ability of seeing them at close range!)

Heaven retired from the world, and **Cronus** (whom the Romans called Saturn) took over Daddy Heaven's business, married his sister **Rhea,** (whom the Romans called Ops) and settled down to being as big a despot as his old man had been!

The old saying, "Like Father, like Son", proved to be completely true in this case, because Cronus just couldn't stand the sight of *his own sons and heirs*. Everytime Rhea gave birth, Cronus – used to pick up the baby, blanket and all, and swallow the lot (without benefit of wine – or water!)

Like all leaders, Cronus realised that the greatest threat to his power, lay within his own camp, so to speak, therefore he concentrated his energies on crushing the revolution before it could blossom! (This may be a mixture of metaphors, but the sense is there if you look carefully enough!)

By about her sixth pregnancy, Rhea was getting pretty sick and tired of the whole thing. After all what was the use of going through nine months of agony and morning-sickness with nothing to show for it at the end? Therefore she hid her sixth born, **Zeus** (Jupiter, in Latin) and when Cronus came in for his evening feed, she gave him a *stone* wrapped up in a blanket – instead of a baby!

Cronus (who was one of those people who eat heartily, but not fastidiously) swallowed it down without noticing the difference, belched happily, and retired to bed.

Much later in time, Zeus (after being aided by this Grandmother Earth and after managing to become Captain of the Gods and Leader of the World) forced his father Cronus to disgorge the stone (along with the five babies) and this piece of inorganic material was eventually set up at Delphi, to be viewed and described by the very first Tourist Writer, **Pausanias,** in 180 A.D.

Quite possibly it could be said that Cronus was the Father of All Digestive Troubles, and Medical Practitioners might care to repeat this story to all their Patients who suffer from ulcers, indigestion, and gastroenteritis. The moral of this tale is obviously, "Eat in haste, and repent at leisure!" ˙

Zeus, very sensibly, stayed hidden in Crete, until he was big and sassy enough to take on Cronus in a war, which rocked the world for many an aeon.

Unfortunately for Cronus, he not only had his son Zeus to contend with in this war, but he had also managed to alienate the affections of his wife, his mother, and his nephew **Prometheus** (who was the son of one of his brother Titans.) Prometheus, incidentally, is one of the few really 'nice guys' in this scenario, and will figure largely in later stories.

Fans of the Television serial "Dallas" will find the ensuing story rather familiar, as Zeus is a typical "J.R." type character, with Cronus playing an aging "Jock Ewing" and worried Mother Earth, like "Miss Elli" spends her time tearing up and down, trying to patch up the world in this troubled period. It is not recorded in Greek Mythology whether Rhea, like "Sue-Ellen", took to the bottle, but if she did, one could hardly blame her, because Zeus turned out to be worse than any of the rulers who came before him!

At the beginning of this battle for control of the world, Zeus very shrewdly released from the bowels of the earth, all those imprisoned monsters such as Thunder, Lightning, and Earthquake; and having formed his Mercenary Army, or "Deities Liberation Group", he unleashed them on his father, Cronus, and achieved a stunning victory.

Having won the war, Zeus did not rest on his laurels, but being an astute politician as well as great military genius, he realised that *the only good enemy is a dead one!* So, like all imperialist leaders ever since, he set about removing all possible opposition from his path.

Everyone who had been against Zeus, was rounded up, including Tartarus, who had sided with Cronus in the War of the Gods and who was now despatched to a solitary labour camp in the bowels of the earth.

Atlas, another enemy, was condemned to spend his existence in eternally holding-up Heaven on his shoulders; which meant that he suffered not only physically from the strain of such exertion, but also had to bear the mental and spiritual anguish of knowing that it was he who was supporting Zeus in all his glory in Heaven! (Heaven, at this point in time, was now a really spectacular mansion, complete with all modern conveniences, somewhere between the sky, and Mt. Olympus in Thessaly, Greece.)

In the punishment meted out to Atlas, and later to others who transgressed the laws of Zeus, it can be seen that the Captain of the Gods was a particularly sadistic character who lacked neither imagination, nor resolution, in devising his torture techniques.

Mother Earth was shocked and disappointed in Zeus' behaviour, and she made one last attempt to get rid of this greedy misuse of power, by giving birth (asexually again) to one more monster, called Typhon.

But now that Zeus had Thunder and Lightning under his control, he wiped the floor with Typhon – figuratively speaking of course.

Typhon retreated to the depths of the earth to sulk and mutter, and to burst forth every now and then, generally in the vicinity of the Earthquake Belt, or wherever he could find a volcanic cone which could be adjusted to fit his wrath.

There were a few more attempted Coups and even a Putsch or two by various Giants who were still around after Typhon had made his valiant effort, but Zeus put down all opposition with the aid of **Hercules,** who was a real tough guy, and just dying to be helpful, and show his patriotism.

Hercules was not actually a bad person, but he used all his tremendous energy for an evil cause, and it is philosophical to note that for all the Zeus type characters of this world, there are always Herculean type characters *who help to keep them in power!* Strong in brawn, but weak in brains, Hercules made a perfect body-guard for a tyrant like Zeus.

Having finally established his right of Tenancy to Heaven, Zeus set about filling the house with furniture, and creating a family, and a dynasty which would continue for ever and ever.

The Palace was not only populated by Zeus and the other eleven Chief Gods and Goddesses, but there were always Muses, Spirits, and lesser Gods visiting, so life was never dull. In fact, Olympus was rather like the average Greek family home of today, with relations continually dropping in for the odd glass of nectar or ambrosia, and everybody getting in everybody else's way!

Mother Earth retired from the battle for justice (as she had lost faith in her off-spring) and contented herself by retreating from the world as much as possible, muttering, "Life is a Jungle!" and "That's what you get from spoiling kids!" Bereft of hope, she closed her eyes and went to sleep to dream of all her past glory, and vanquished aspirations.

THE CREATION OF MEN

As yet there were no humans in this world which was now free of all monsters, and which possessed only beautiful, glamourous Gods just waiting to be adored. As the Gods got rather tired of each other; and as it is not very satisfying for a God to be adored by another God; they invented Man!

There are many stories concerning the Creation of Man, and the Reader must simply believe that which he prefers. Most people only believe what they *choose* to believe anyway! The Truth is an extremely strong potion, and probably should only be taken in small doses, for fear it will kill more than it will cure.

Creation Story No. 1

Prometheus (whose name means Provider, and also Forethought) was a really clever good and Titan, but he had a brother called Epimetheus (meaning Afterthought) who was *not as intelligent, nor as wise.*

For some reason or other, **Epimetheus** was given the job of creating both animals and men, and for some reason best known to himself, he decided to do a better job on the animals – than on the men!

Seeing he had such a love for animals, it seems strange that Epimetheus has not been used as a symbol on the notepaper of animal protection societies, but then maybe animal lovers don't ever brother to read Greek Mythology, and hence know nothing about him.

Anyway, the crux of the matter is that Epithemeus gave all the best gifts of the Gods to the animals. He gave them strength, cunning, courage, fur, feathers, beauty of form and voice, and much, much more. By the time he had finished however, *there wasn't anything left for him to give to Man!*

Prometheus realised what a mess his brother had made of the whole thing, so he took over the contract and tried to see what he could do to straighten things out.

Firstly he did some reconstruction work on Men, and gave them a better shape – so that even though they didn't have any other virtues, at least they looked better than the animals did, and would prove to be of greater inspiration to sculptors in the years to come. (If Prometheus hadn't done this, then Tourists today might go flocking into Museums to see statues of dogs and cats, instead of Discus Throwers, and Dying Gladiators.)

Then Prometheus went up to Heaven, and rooted around in Zeus' fire-place until he had a nicely burning piece of wood which he brought down and gave to the first men, so that at least they could keep their naked selves warm, and manage to barbecue their food in the evenings.

Naturally Zeus was furious with Prometheus, because Fire was supposed to be the special province of the Gods, and when Mortals possessed it, they began to share some of the secrets of the Immortals, and began to think themselves *the equals of their betters!*

It could be said in Marxist terminology that Prometheus committed "Class Suicide" in order to help the "Masses", and like all the people who have followed his action throughout the centuries, he suffered mightily for his high principles, and has long been forgotten by the very people whom he attempted to help.

SUCH IS THE FATE OF ALL HUMANITARIANS!

Therefore Dear Reader, if you are humanely inclined, GIVE IT UP! – Or else *You too, will suffer as Prometheus did!* (The Writer of this Guide, speaks from experience in this matter!)

Creation Story No. 2

In this version of the Creation, *ALL THE GODS created Man.* But they experimented with various chemical mixtures until they finally decided on the particularly poisonous brew of which we are the remnants.

The First Race of Men which the Gods created were men made of Gold.

These were happy, intelligent, beautiful and pure spirits who all passed out of this world to become some 'Blessed Dead', inhabiting some other land far removed from this world.

Why exactly such intelligent and good people should all disappear is not told us, but they did, and that is why the Gods had to start creating all over again.

The Second Race of Men which the Gods turned out, were made of Silver, and were not a patch on the Men of Gold.

They had little intelligence, and seemed to love hurting each other, with the result that they killed each other off. When they died – as they didn't have any spirits (due to their being such aggressive idiots!) it was not necessary to send their 'shades' anywhere and they just ceased to exist!

It may seem weird but the Gods kept right on experimenting, and experimenting with baser metals as well because the Third Race of Men were made from Brass, and they were the lowest human forms of all!

They were extremely violent, and absolutely adored war, and all forms of cruelty, so the world didn't have them for long, as they murdered each other in an extraordinarily short time, and it was probably a good thing too! (One wonders of course, whether there are any of them still around nowadays – especially when one reads the international news!)

After this fiasco, and just as the Gods were obviously beginning to doubt their own deification, they struck 'pay dirt' as a Miner might say, because they managed to construct a race of men who were valiant, heroic, and beautiful; who loved adventures, and glorious wars (exactly what the difference was between a 'glorious' war, and any other type of war, they don't say) and these were the heroes of Ancient Greece as are portrayed in Homer's Iliad.

These glorious warriors all died off as well (after all, being a Warrior for a living can hardly be considered as safe as being a

Clerk in an Insurance Company!) but when these warriors left the world, they went to a place of perfect bliss, where they lived like the Gods themselves, and drank themselves silly on nectar, and such like duty free alcohol.

Now that the Fourth Race had all disappeared from the scene, the Gods completely lost their heads (and their touch) and created the Fifth Race who were made of Iron.

The Iron Race were *extremely evil* (and still are, because we are included in this lot!) *WITH EVERY SON WORSE THAN HIS FATHER BEFORE HIM!* Might was Right to them, and they worshipped power, and thirsted for blood. (Although the majority of them are so terrible however, there have been known to be occasional slip-ups in the genetic banks, and some of them have almost managed to be compassionate and helpful to each other!)

Zeus took one look at them, and decided that when finally in this world, there is no man existing who is angered at the wrong doing and injustice that he sees; and when there is no one to feel shame at the misery all around him; then He, Zeus, will finally, and once and for all time, destroy the whole damn lot of them, and be finished with Human Beings for all time!

There is a proviso in the Will though, which reads, *that the World could change, if, the common people arose to destroy their oppressors.* Obviously this thought has spurred on many an anarchist all through history.

No matter how these stories of Creation differ, they are identical in one respect, and that is, that in every one of them, *there are NO WOMEN!*

Doubtless it was this lack of *Female Companionship,* which led to all those dreary fights, and bloodthirsty battles which the Races of Men kept having. It takes a woman, and a television set, to keep a man at home – and happy! Ancient Man had neither.

As the origins of Men are somewhat open to debate, so it is with Women. There are two main stories concerning the Creation of them.

The Creation of Women Story No. 1

As Zeus was furious with Prometheus for giving Fire to Men (and thereby making them more clever and more comfortable than they had any right to be) he decided to revenge himself on Man, by giving him *WOMAN*.

It must also be noted that Prometheus not only gave Men fire, but he also annoyed Zeus by tricking him into agreeing to accept only the fat and bones of animal sacrifices, and leaving the best parts of the carcasses for Men.

At this period in time, it seems that when early man sacrificed animals (or possibly people!) to the Gods, he gave them the whole corpse. The Iconoclast may care to speculate to himself on how fat and well-fed the priests in the temples must have been during this epoch, because the Mythology assures us that the Gods *Only* indulged in **Nectar** and **Ambrosia,** so one wonders exactly, *WHO WAS EATING THE STEAK?*

Whatever the truth of the situation is, it is said that Zeus used to accept the *whole body* of the animal, and that Prometheus swindled him one day, by putting the meat into one bundle, and the fat and bones into another.

He then offered the two bundles to Zeus, and asked him which one he preferred, and warned him, that from that time on, he would *ONLY* receive that which he had selected.

Zeus (who seems to have been rather stupid for such an almighty and all powerful figure) chose the bundle of bones and fat. He chose it because it *looked larger,* and because it *smelt more delicious,* which goes to prove how little he knew about nutrition, and food in general!

When Zeus discovered how he had been cheated, his fury new no bounds, and cursing fit to burst, he stamped off to find the other Gods to help him create '*PANDORA*'.

Pandora (whose name means the 'gifts of all the Gods') was extremely beautiful, but also extremely *EVIL,* and it is recorded that from the day she came down on earth, *ALL the Troubles of the World Started!*

110

It seems a little hard to believe that *One Woman* could have been the cause of *ALL* the World Wars, Nuclear Bombs, Racial Hatred, Social Unrest, air and water Pollution and Criminality which we enjoy today – but it is so! The Mythology tells us that until she appeared on the scene, men were *completely without dissension!*

Personally I think that men credit women with more intelligence and ability than they, they the women, *actually possess!* Even if Pandora had never come on earth, I'm sure men would have found some ingenious way to discover evil for themselves – *without any help from the Weaker Sex!*

The Creation of Women Story No. 2

In this story, the reasons for creating women are exactly the same as in the previous one, but Pandora is not a particularly evil woman, only a *Curious* one!

It is fairly true to state that in women, Curiosity is more highly developed, but then most sociologists, psychologists and anthropologists state that 'Curiosity' is a sign of intelligence in *all animals,* and therefore the first step, or basic essential needed for the progress of Life and/or Civilization. I will leave it to the Reader to decide if 'Curiosity' really equals 'Intelligence', and if it does, then the Reader must also decide if Women, being more Curious, are in consequence more Intelligent than Men!

Anyway, the Gods created beautiful Pandora, and sent her to earth, clutching a box, which they had forbidden her to open.

Of course *We* all know that the box contained everthing *EVIL! But how was poor Pandora to know?*

Zeus realised that she would probably open the box one day, simply due to boredom, and he thought of the most boring life that he could give her, and finally decided to send her to be the wife (i.e. house-wife) of Epimetheus.

Prometheus warned his brother not to accept gifts from Zeus as they were likely to be as bad as the Giver Himself, and here we have the original saying which the Trojans later discovered to be true - "Beware of Greeks bearing Gifts!"

111

In this instance however, it was "Beware of Greek Gods bearing Gifts!" but Epimetheus disregarded the advice of Prometheus, and learned to this sorrow at a later stage, how very right his brother had been all along!

(When Wisdom comes in such a way as this, it is often difficult to fully appreciate, as it is so tinged with remorse; and Epimetheus must have muttered regretfully to himself, "Experience is a Hard School, but Fools will learn in no other!" In much the same way, the Trojans probably felt after having ignored the advice of Cassandra, and having seen their city destroyed.But then a prophet is never recognised in his own country – *or, in his own home!*

Although Epimetheus loved Pandora passionately, he left her alone at home a great deal of the time, while he was busy talking politics with the other men in the local coffee shops.

She (very naturally) became bored, as did Eve in the Garden of Eden at a later period in history. Women need a large amount of attention from their men, in order for them not to begin thinking and developing their brains. *Men just never seem to realise this!*

Just as Eve started to look at the apple tree, so Pandora started to look at the box, and as woman is a less slavish creature than man, she thought to herself, "Why the heck shouldn't I open it?" So, she gave in to the impulse; lifted the lid; and for the first time, the world was filled with plague, war, sickness, despair, inflation, unemployment, recession, and all the other economic ills which threaten us now, and to which we have grown accustomed.

But, along with all the horrors which floated throughout the world there came one good thing; and that was *HOPE*. (Although one would have to be extremely optimistic to believe that *Hope alone,* could deal with all the misery mentioned above!)

But this story of Pandora proves the Biological and Evolutionary law, that for every Disadvantage, there is an Advantage (and of course vice versa!) And this theory also *proved* the *Power of the Gods;* and Men realised that they could not outsmart them, and that they'd better give up trying, because *the System always won!*

Having finished punishing Man by giving him Woman, Zeus turned his attention to Prometheus, as he was not only a source of constant irritation to Zeus, but also a *Real Danger. Who knew when Prometheus might not raise some sort of Revolution against the Gods, and help Man to TAKE OVER HEAVEN!*

Force and Violence, the servants of Zeus, were sent to arrest Prometheus, and they took him to a mountain peak high in the Caucasus, where they bound him to a rock, with chains which would never break. Then Zeus sent an eagle to feast on Prometheus' body, which it would continue to do unceasingly, for All Eternity!

All of this you might think was more than enough, but Zeus wasn't finished yet! He *Knew* that Prometheus *Knew,* that one day there would come into the world, a child, who would grow up to take the power from Zeus, and eventually dethrone him.

Zeus wanted to know the name of the Woman who was destined to give birth to this child (presumably so he could have her sterilised, or fixed in some way!)

Hermes (the sneaky, cheating God of Commerce) was sent to soft-soap Prometheus, and to promise him his freedom from the horrors of his torture, if only he would co-operate with the authorities and inform!

Here we see the 'Hard Cop, Soft Cop' routine tried out in the world for the first time, with Hermes attempting to soften up the prisoner, in order to get the information. But it didn't meet with any success with Prometheus. Prometheus was *Bound in Body, but Free in Spirit, and he refused to parley with Hermes.* Except to tell him to go back and tell his master Zeus, that he would never give in!

Then Hermes showed his real face, and cursed, and swore, and declared that Prometheus was mad to prefer suffering and high principles to a life of luxury in Olympus, with Ambrosia and

Nectar constantly on tap. (Hermes was the type who could never have undertood any type of principle or idealism, and would have gladly *sold his own mother six times over — if only he could have been really sure who she was!)*

So Prometheus chose to stay there, and suffer until this day – the God of the Underdog, and the symbol of rebellion against all injustice, and the authority of power!

There is a later story in Mythology, that Hercules used his sling to kill the eagle that was eating Prometheus, and that Zeus still declared that Prometheus could not be freed until some other deity would consent to take his place on the rocks.

An even later story is that Chiron, a Centaur, gave his life in order that Prometheus be freed. But this is a rather spurious tale, and one gets the impression that probably these later stories were invented for the sentimental and the squeamish, who didn't like to think that there weren't happy endings for everyone!

There is yet another story regarding the Creation of Mankind, and that is the story of the 'Stone People'.

It begins with a 'Deluge', which seems to have been popular with so many people in mythology (not to mention geographers, who like to use this point to prove the existence of an 'Ice Age', and the melting of same.)

The story goes this way. The Men on earth were so wicked that Zeus got really tired of them, and determined to destroy them, so he sent a flood (naturally with the aid of his brother Poseidon, the God of the Sea, who is called Neptune, in Latin.)

The world – apart from Parnassus in Greece – was covered in water, because it had rained for nine days and nine nights.

A large box (the Greek version of the 'Ark', drifted to the top of Parnassus, and inside were **Deucalion,** the son of Prometheus, and his wife, Pyrrha, the daughter of Pandora and Epimetheus.

Prometheus, being such a wise and capable Titan, had told these two, to build the floating box, and to stay in it until the rain stopped. Unlike Noah, he did not mention anything about livestock, but then probably the Greeks were never great animal lovers, as is evinced by their attitude to dogs and cats. Or maybe these two were newly married, and fancied that they could live on LOVE ALONE!

When the water started to drain away, Pyrrha and Deucalion came down from Parnassus as the only living beings, on the entire earth. They found a water-logged and soggy temple still standing at the base of the mountain, so they decided to go in and give thanks for their safe deliverance.

Rather late in the day, metaphorically speaking, Zeus decided to feel sorry for them, and he sent down disembodied voices to speak to Pyrrha and Deucalion. (Doubtless the reason these voices were disembodied, was because none of the celestial beings in Olympus wanted to get their feet wet!) Anyhow, these disembodied voices of water-fearing Gods, told the couple, to cast behind them the bones of their mother.

Pyrrha got very upset on hearing this order, and is reputed to have said, "Never would I do such a thing!"

The words used in the mythology are definitely "Would", and not "Could", so one must suppose that Pyrrha was carrying around the bones of her mother with her, in the box, for nine days and nine nights! (This seems in itself to be a pretty gruesome sort of hobby – but each to his own taste!)

Deucalion however, thought it over logically, and reasoned that their mother was in actual fact, the Earth! So he said, "It's alright! We can just throw some stones over our shoulders. That should do the trick".

So they did. And as the stones fell on the earth, they turned into People, and a New Human Race began.

This is a nice little story, and it goes to prove that anything was possible to the Ancient Greeks, because in the stories of Creation, we have traversed the whole range of Reproduction Techniques, from Sexual, Asexual, and Bisexual, to Inorganic and Organic.

Obviously the Moral of all Greek Mythological Reproduction was, "Where there is a Will, there is a Way!"

CHAPTER VI

THE DISPOSSESSED OLD GREEK NATURE GODS
AND VEGETATION DEITIES AND
THE BIRTH OF THE GREEK THEATRE

All ancient societies at one stage in their civilization believed in Vegetation Deities, as these ancient people were mainly agricultural beings, whose very lives depended on the whims of Nature. Therefore the first Gods in any of the primitive tribes were generally the Sun, then the Moon, and after this, the Earth itself; as the Earth was the Mother of All Life Forms. Following on from this there grew up an attachment to, and special cults, regarding certain crops which were necessary for survival, and which were symbolic in their growth cycles.

With the arrival of the Aristocracy of Thessaly, the rise of the City-State, Commerce, and a Systematized Life-Style (with a place for everything, and everything in its place) the old Vegetation Gods lost their power and only remained venerable in the minds of the peasants in the country.

The peasants of course never counted for anything then (or, indeed now!) as they were only regarded as necessary to grow the food to feed the people in the cities. Peasants never have had any social standing whatsoever, in fact they may be deemed even lower than teachers, who are considered to be another 'untouchable caste'. We all eat the food of the farm labourer but seldom spare him a thought; and if we do think about him, then it's bound to be in an unkind and disparaging way. (The Law of Life seems to be that the more you produce, and the more essential is your service, the less you are repaid, or respected for it!)

There has always been a conflict between the City and the Country, and it has its roots in the Ancient Greek Civilization.

116

The Cities developed New Gods to go with their new power, and the peasants and the land-locked population, were pushed down under the change-over, stamped on once or twice, and then forgotten about.

So it came about that the Old Gods lost their powers, and as there was no room in Olympus for them, they became rather secondary adjuncts and formed the basis for cults attached to the main religion.

Later though, towards the end of the Greek Empire, one of the Old Gods suddenly became very popular for reasons neither agricultural nor religious, and he was worshipped more manifestly than any of the other Olympians, so that a new background had to be created for him – in order to put him up in Olympus with the rest!

The oldest Vegetation Deity was Demeter (known as Ceres, in Latin) and she was the Goddess of Corn, and the daughter of Cronus and Rhea. She became associated with the idea of Mother Nature Herself, although in fact she was not, as Earth (or Nature) had retired many years previously and was spending her dotage and declining years in lonely solitude, like an unwanted grandmother in an Old Peoples' Home.

Demeter's Temples were the threshing floors and the fields themselves, which goes to show that she could never have hoped to compete with the Temples of the Olympians. Whoever heard of a God or Goddess of any Consequence, being worshipped in a barn?

Her chief festival was at harvest time in Autumn, or at the Sowing of the Seed in Spring, which festival we now call Easter. People baked new bread and consecrated it to her, and sacrificed young children in the fields so that the crops would grow faster and richer with all that good mineral content from sweet, young blood, seeping into them!

In certain Agricultural and Developing countries in the world today, people still attach a great deal of significance to 'Easter

Bread', and this is a spiritual hang-over from the days of Demeter's power. Unfortunately though, in an Industrially inclined world (not to mention a Technologically crazy one!) Demeter has no real business to do today, besides sitting around the offices of the United Nations in New York, and trying to advise on agricultural policies in the 3rd World. (Needless to relate, nobody takes any notice of her!)

Even after the advent of the Twelve Great Gods in Olympus, Demeter still had a rather influential temple at Eleusis, near Athens, which must have been a type of agricultural area akin to an early Kansas in the U.S.A.

Here in Eleusis, every five years, was held the **Eleusinian Mysteries** Festival, and this festival which lasted for nine days in September, dealt with secret ceremonies concerning the Life and Death Cycle.

As no archaeologist or classical scholar seems to know exactly what was going on at this festival, we may therefore assume that it was some type of Agricultural State Fair, combined with a lot of religious 'hocus pocus' and 'mumbo jumbo'!

Dionysos (Bacchus, in Latin) the **God of Grapes, and Wine,** was also one of the old **Vegetation Deities,** and was likewise worshipped at **Eleusis,** along with Demeter.

People drank wine made from the new grapes of the Mediterranean region, and celebrated these two unhappy Gods, and Divinities of Earth – who like people, suffered from the cold environment in the winter, and like people (who did not have to pay for internal or external heating in the warmer months) rose to a new and happy life again each summer.

Demeter was the older of the Earth Divinites, as corn was planted and used long before men discovered how to anaesthetize themselves with drink. Some people may of course dispute this point, and say that wine is far more necessary to survival than bread, and therefore Dionysos should have been worshipped long before Demeter. But anyone who has ever gotten drunk on an empty stomach will tell you that bread is

Bacchus: by Titian

absolutely indispensable, and that *after* it, comes wine. Bread means survival, and wine means happiness; but in order to be happy, one must first survive!

According to the Myths, Demeter was in fact the sister of Zeus, and she had a daughter **Persephone (Proserpine,** in Latin) who was the maiden of Spring.

One day, when Persephone was dancing around in the fields, enjoying the sun, and creating the flowers; sex-crazy, and love-starved Pluto, saw her, and abducted her to his home in the Nether Regions of the world.

Demeter searched for her daughter for nine days (the same time span as the Eleusinian Mysteries) until finally the Sun told her where Persephone was, and then **Demeter** became so angry and disenchanted with the whole God System, that she decided to leave Olympus and take up residence on earth like any mere mortal. She completely gave up worrying over her Divine Duties and Committments, and, like a King who abdicates, she left her people to the mercies of the politicians, i.e. crafty **Zeus** and Company.

She landed on Earth in the village of Eleusis, and was taken in by a family of women who felt sorry for this poor, strange, mad woman with a brow creased in grief and sorrow. There in Eleusis, Demeter occupied herself by looking after a child (the baby of the family in which she was staying) and to whom she had taken a fancy – due no doubt to the loss of her own daughter to Pluto.

One night in order to immortalize the baby, she tried to lay him in the fire, but his real mother suddenly came in the room, caught her in the act, and screamed and took on so, that Demeter was forced to reveal herself as a Goddess; and not just a crazy, child-hungry old woman.

The baby incidentally was not burnt (neither did he become immortal, due to the interruption in the immortal making process) however he was honoured all his life in Eleusis, and could never walk down the main street, without people pointing

120

and saying, "Oh, Look! There goes whats-his-name, the one who was nearly an Olympian!"

As Eleusis is not especially mentioned in any of the history books (or recorded in any of the important annals of civilization) we can safely assume that this incident was their *only* fleeting flirtation with glory, and they – simple people that they were – were very grateful for it!

The people of Eleusis were instructed by Demeter to build her a temple near the city centre, and Demeter sat down in this temple and spent her entire time crying and wailing, and generally wasting away, in longing for her daughter down in Hades.

Everything in nature began to waste away as well, because now that Demeter wasn't minding her business, and seeing to the fields, the whole world started going to pieces and Famine struck everywhere. As Demeter was experiencing a nervous breakdown, so was the world, and as the City-States needed to eat the food of the despised peasants, so things became extremely difficult for them, and for the Olympians, who had to put with the insults of the people in the urban areas down below.

Zeus began to fear that a revolution might occur, so he sent down some of the other Gods to plead with Demeter to stop her strike action and to go back to work. But Demeter wouldn't even bother to *negotiate!* She stated flatly that the earth would bear no fruit until she had seen her daughter.

What could Zeus do in these circumstances? After all, the Captain of the Gods could hardly be expected to have any knowledge concerning anything as common or garden as growing food! He usually spent all his time lazing around Olympus, seducing women, or sending bolts of lightning down on unfortunate people's heads. How could he suddenly start rolling up his sleeves, and applying himself to anything as vulgar as the hoe or the plough, at this late stage in his life?

"But I'm a White-collar Worker, and a Big Business Executive," Zeus said. "What on earth can I do to rectify this food shortage? After all, Demeter has worked in the fields all her life. It's *different* for her. Good Heavens, what would happen to my hands? And I have my back to think of as well! Really, she's making things so difficult. How can the Captain of the Gods, and the most Important Being in the Universe be expected to go down and do anything which might be termed useful? Why, I'd lose my Image, and my Subjects' Respect!"

So Zeus decided he would have to concede to Demeter's demands, and he sent Hermes down to the Underworld, to tell Pluto to surrender Persephone, and return her to her mother, who was proving more troublesome than an International Dock-Workers' Strike.

Hermes found Persephone sitting down in Hades in a spirit of deep resentment; bitter about life in general; and refusing to even look at Pluto – let alone share his nuptial couch! Pluto himself was standing near the fire in embarrassed confusion like a man who has brought home a new colour television set, only to find that the electricity has been cut off, because he forgot to pay his bill.

"O.K." said Hermes, "Zeus says that you're to go home to your mother right away, because he can't put up with the condition of the world any longer. *And you, Pluto,* must just learn to live with it! Zeus is your older brother, and the Captain of the Gods, and you'll have to abide by what he says!"

Rather strangely (and peculiarly rapidly also) Pluto agreed, but he insisted on giving Persephone a 'pomegranate' seed to eat before she departed, in order to strengthen her for the long journey.

Unbeknownst to Persephone, the 'pomegranate' seed had strange powers, and her eating it meant that she would have to return to Hades every year, for four months of the year. Why exactly pomegranates should be so powerful, no one knows, or if they do, then they haven't bothered to inform the rest of us. But it is plain that pomegranates are a dangerous fruit, and personally speaking, the author *never liked them* — even as a small child!

Probably the basis of the whole story lies in the fact that nobody would really like a perpetual spring and summer, because to have too much of a good thing, gets you down! If people didn't have winter (to shiver through) and summer (to look forward to) then they wouldn't know what to do with themselves! Good and bad are only relative anyway, and how would you know that anything was good if you never had some unpleasant experience with which to compare it?

So Persephone and Demeter were re-united. But Demeter was still unhappy because Persephone would have to return to Hades for one quarter of the year, and therefore Demeter didn't feel like giving her abundant energies to the World Agricultural Five-Year-Plan.

Troubled Zeus, decided finally to send his mother **Rhea to** beg and plead with Demeter to return to work, before the world had completely, agriculturally, expired!

"After all", said Rhea, "Persephone is the daughter of Zeus as well as yourself (this was in fact true, as Zeus was always having relationships with his sisters because he believed in 'Line Breeding' for quality, as the Dog Fanciers call it) and he only wanted *the best for her!* This arranged marriage between Persephone and Pluto is really a great opportunity, and Persephone will be the Queen of the Underworld, and hold a position much envied by many another girl!"

Demeter was still going to refuse the deal, but, she looked about the earth, and suddenly felt so sorry for the people in their suffering and hunger, that she decided to return to Olympus and to take up her duties once more.

Before she left Earth however, she taught the people of Eleusis how to sow corn and do other useful things with the soil, in order to eke out a living. (One wonders what on earth they were eating before she arrived on the scene. Could it have been that they were only existing on berries and wild fruits?)

This story proves though, that although Demeter lived in Olympus, she was really associated with the Earth and mortals.

123

She represented sorrowing Motherhood; the Land; and Old Agricultural Societies; i.e. all the old traditions which had been swept away by the new City-States, and the glamourous New Gods of the New, City-State, orientated Religion.

Dionysos or Bacchus, was the last God to enter Olympus. In all his writing, Homer, didn't even admit to his presence or existence, but stories grew up concerning him by various other writers and story-tellers; and later Dionysos became a very convenient God for the Establishment, because he was a very popular God with all types of people.

This is not surprising when one considers that alcohol is popular with most classes of society – The only difference being that if you are poor, then you're a 'drunk' and if you're rich, then you can be an 'alcoholic'. Being an alcoholic, 'drying-out', in an expensive clinic, is naturally definitely superior to being a poor drunk, in the gutter; or a poor drunk, 'drying-out', in the cell of a City Police Station.

According to legend, Dionysos was born in Thebes, and was the son of Zeus, and a Theban princess called **Semele**. He was the only god whose parents were *not* both divine, and therefore being half plebian, was consequently popular with the plebs of earth. The Greek Religious System only admitted Dionysos into the Olympian Establishment at a time when the 'Establishments' of the various Greek City States (Athens in particular) were having a very hard time keeping control and balancing their power, and when they needed to encourage people to drink vast quantities of alcohol in order to make them courageous enough (or stupid enough) to fight for the ever expanding Greek Empire.

Semele, the mother of the God of Wine, was a very unfortunate woman; because although Zeus was madly in love with her (as he was with every other woman he met!) he was instrumental in killing her because of his deeply passionate love.

Zeus had sworn an oath by the River Styx (an oath which we are led to believe even *He* could not break; and it is comforting to

124

know that even Gods have honour, and that there are some things which even they can do nothing about!) And this oath was, that whatever, Semele asked of him, he would do!

Semele said that what she most desired was to see Zeus fully rigged out in his splendid robes as the King of Heaven and Lord of the Thunderbolt!

Now, as his Numero Uno mistress, she could have asked for many other things, as for example: – a Penthouse on Fifth Avenue; a new diamond ring; a Mazzerati Sports Car; or even a Greek Island of her very own! But none of these however seemed to catch her fancy, and so she didn't ask for *any* of them. She had this insane desire to see Zeus in all his glory; and being such a stupid woman, we can say that she probably deserved to die, and in fact, maybe *needed to die;* and even had some type of "Death Wish", which had developed from a depressing and psychologically bad childhood! Because according to mythology, it was written that, *no mortal could see Zeus all dressed up like that, and still live after the experience.* So Semele was *asking for it!*

Also, Zeus knew quite well that when he got himself all togged up and stood before her, she would rapidly dematerialize, and yet he didn't really try to dissuade her, so probably he was just as happy to get rid of her anyway; as he always tired of his various sweethearts quite early on in these affairs.

Naturally though, the whole idea of seeing Zeus dressed in this way had been put into Semele's head by *Hera,* who was thirsting to lay waste to one of Zeus' paramours. No mistress in her right mind would have asked for anything as ridiculous and boring as Semele had done!

Zeus, having sworn to agree to her commands, appeared in his garments of burning, blinding, light; whereupon Semele died immediately, and her soul went down to the Underworld, for the Boatman to carry into Hades. Just before she went however, Zeus (who knew that she was with child) performed a neat 'Caesarian Section' on Semele as she was drawing her last breath, and placed the baby inside himself, to be born six months later.

When one reads this sort of rubbish (like Zeus carrying a baby about inside himself) one begins to wonder if the Greeks *actually knew the "Facts of Life" at all!* Of course, one must not overlook the possibility that maybe the ancients were all **Hermaphroditic,** and therefore more highly advanced than ourselves in this matter! (Anyway, the Greeks were never ones for letting Logic stand in the way of a good story – and this is a *remarkably good story!)*

After Dionysos was born, and came forth from the belly of his father, Zeus gave him to Hermes, who in turn, gave him to a group of Nymphs of Nysa, who lived in the sky as a constellation of stars which brought the rain.

Nymphs in those times were really rather loose-living creatures as the Author has explained previously, and were in some ways approximate to the 'Call-Girls' of our time. So we can therefore say with some moral rectitude that Hermes did not exactly pick a suitable environment for a young boy to be brought-up in. But the story does suit mythology because by it is proved that the God of Wine was born of Fire (Zeus in his shining glory) and nursed by Rain (the Nymphs) and that is how grapes are made! Furthermore, as everyone in those days seems to have been 'loose-living', the Nymphs were probably no worse than anyone else; and wherever Dionysos had lived, and with whom, the effect would most likely have been the same.

When he was old enough, Dionysos left this brothel in the sky, and Hippie-like, he wandered round the world, teaching people, not to smoke hash and get high, but to grow grapes and get drunk!

He went to Lydia, Phrygia, Persia, Medes and Araby, and everywhere people flocked to him, listened, and drank, and blessed his name. Only in Greece was he unknown, because there, people still drank water; or tried to distill corn whiskey; or just put up with life as it was; and went to bed early to sleep their troubles away!

During his journeys around the Mediterranean, some Greek Pirates (thinking that he was the son of a rich man) kid-napped him, and carried him aboard their ship to hold him for ransome.

But they shouldn't have done it, because suddenly the ship was becalmed, and grape vines grew all over the place; and the Captain and the crew turned into dolphins, and threw themselves over-board at the sight of their captive who had suddenly changed into a lion, and who was advancing on them, over the wine-wet decks.

It is not recorded what happened after this, but possibly the reason why Dolphins are considered to be such intelligent creatures is simply because they are really the souls of Ancient Greek sailors, who even today, are still trying to communicate to us the terrible experiences they underwent a couple of thousand years ago. (Zoologists might care to investigate this theory.)

Dionysos also passed through Thrace on his way to Greece, and was insulted while there, by the **King Lycurgus,** who opposed this new worship of the vine, and who was some type of early Puritan or Prohibitionist. Therefore Dionysos imprisoned the said Prohibitionist in a cave, without any water (let alone wine) and cursed him with a continual burning thirst and maddening rage.

Then Zeus got interested in the case, and decided to likewise revenge this show of bad manners to his son, and he struck the poor man blind!

Lycurgius died soon after this, which was really just as well, considering the condition he was in, and Dionysos continued on his happy drunk-sodden way to Naxos.

In Naxos, he came across the Princess **Ariadne** of Crete, who had been abandoned by the Athenian Prince **Theseus,** and left sitting on the shore alone and forlorn like the proverbial pebble.

(This is actually just another version of the old, old story of men playing women false, and is very like the drama of **Jason** and

Ariadne resting

Medea. The Ancient Greek Males were always very happy to have the help of foreign females in their travels, *but,* when it came time to bring them home to meet the folks, they couldn't for the life of them understand what the erstwhile attraction had been! *How could they ruin their lives, by marrying some foreign penniless girl — when back home, a girl from a good family with a Big Dowry was waiting faithfully for them?*)

Ariadne was the daughter of Minos, the King of Crete, who had a **Labyrinth** there, in which he kept putting people to be eaten by the **Minotaur.** Ariadne had helped Theseus to escape from this fate of being fodder for the Minotaur, and in gratitude he had taken her on his ship bound for Greece, but then changed his mind; put her off at Naxos; and left her there.

Theseus said that Ariadne had been sea-sick, and that, *that* was why he put her on dry land; and that when it came time to go,

Theseus killing the Minotaur: by Poll Ajuolo

he forgot to tell her; or else, that he couldn't find her; or some such lie. But not even an idiot could, or would, believe such a tale! (Gentlemen tourists from all over the world have been trying to leave their wives abandoned and unnoticed in Naxos for years, and *NONE* of them has *ever succeeded!* It is an extremely difficult operation to depart gracefully from the port of Naxos, whistling a gay tune; and pretending to be oblivious of a person waving and screaming hysterically at you from the shore!)

In order to convince the Reader what an utter swine this Theseus was, let me add, that after leaving Ariadne on the shore alone (with-out even any Travellers' Cheques!) he married her sister **Phaedra;** and sexually-starved *her* into madness; so that to compensate, she fell in love with his son **Hippolytus;** and then suffering an attack of morality and guilt, she finally killed herself in despair!

This Hippolytus incidentally was a prude who would never have attracted Phaedra in the first place, if she hadn't been so depressed; and he was the son of Theseus by another foreign woman (an Amazon) whom Theseus had raped on an earlier occasion in his jauntings around the world.

In other words, if the Women's Movement had been around at the time of the Ancients Greeks, this Theseus would have been awarded so many M.C.P. (Male Chauvinist Pig) Ties, that he could have garrotted himself with ease!

It is recorded that Dionysos gave compassion to Ariadne – who knows, perhaps it means that she drank herself to death! Anyhow, she found contentment in the grape, and Dionysos loved her, and gave her a special crown; and after she had died from too much booze and a vitamin E deficiency, he took back the crown and placed it among the stars. At least it can be said that Ariadne died happy – which is more than can be said for most of the people who lived during her period in history.

After this painful and short-lived love affair, Dionysos went down to the Underworld; found his mother; and took her up to Olympus to live with the Gods.

The Olympians were not terribly happy about having a mortal living with them, but they had to make the best of the situation due to the popularity of Dionysos in the world in general. One supposes anyhow, that they put Semele to work in the kitchen, and tried to pretend that she didn't exist – except for the times when Dionysos was in the house of course.

This trip to the Underworld to retrieve his mother proves that Dionysos and wine, are stronger than Death itself, and that anything is possible with a few glasses of something under one's belt. Dionysos therefore became associated on earth with a Life-Death Resurrection Cult because of his vegetation origin, and because of the stories which were told about him – especially this one concerning his mother. And like Demeter, he was the God of the Unhappy, and there were always plenty of psychologically depressed people around in Greece in order to keep this cult going at full strength. Life in Ancient Greece was not exactly a bed of roses, and when the Greeks weren't fighting the Persians or some other foreigners, then they were tearing each other to pieces in the Peloponnesian War, or in other nasty little skirmishes between the City-States. Besides these wars, there were also Religious Persecutions of **Atheists** or Free-Thinkers-like Socrates and others–who were either put to death; banished; or left to rot in gaol.

By the time of **Pericles** (the so-called **"Golden Age"** of Greece) in the 5th Century B.C., there must have been many desperate people about who would have welcomed a drink. Athens at this stage was in its zenith, and supreme among the City-States in the Greek Empire, and yet only a few hundred years away from conquest by Rome. The moral of this being that the *the higher one rises,* the *more rapidly one falls!*

In this glorious artistic Athens there were many slaves who had absolutely no rights whatsoever, and who could look forward to nothing better in life than being able to drink their sorrows away on a few occasions. (Things haven't really changed very much today, because there are many industrial workers in European city-centers who feel exactly the same way – and only wish the Governments would abolish the tax on alcohol so they could manage to get as drunk as the Ancient Greeks did!)

Besides the slaves, there were the **'Metics',** or Foreigners who had settled in Athens, and although not in possession of Greek Citizenship, or any rights (Human or otherwise!) they were allowed to run small businesses in the way that certain foreigners are allowed to own delicatessens and such like in the large European cities of our day. The Metics also worked in Trade, and helped the Athenians to corner the markets in other countries.

131

Higher up the social scale came the **'Demos'**, from which the word **Democracy** is formed. This class included pure Greek Born Athenians who were farmers, artisans, traders, and sailors, and they enjoyed civil rights, but no real political rights. Although the word Democracy is supposed to mean the ruling of the country by the 'Demos', or people, it really was a misnomer, because the Demos did not actually rule at all.

The only really influential group in the City–States which had any power was the **'Eupatrids'** or the people of Good Family, or Good Patriots; and naturally they were the *oldest wealthiest, and most unprincipled families in the place!* (Yes, Dear Reader, you're quite right – things haven't changed at all. It's just the same old story today!)

Therefore out of a possible population of some 300.000, only 40.000 adult males held the power, and that was enough to make anyone want to get drunk!

The Gods of Olympus had always been the mouthpiece of the State, yet most of the people could not identify with them, because while they, the people, led wretched dreary lives of war, and work–the Gods, never knew the meaning of the word sorrow. Dionysos therefore became immensely popular (as he had secretly always been with the peasants) and he began to personify the common man of both the City and the Country, because Dionyos was half-mortal as well as being a God – and because he had had his taste of trouble in his life!

By the 5th Century B.C. also, the Philosophical Thought of Miletus had finally taken root securely in Athens, and the more intellectual of the Greeks began to wonder if Olympus and the exploits of Zeus were all that there was to life. The word **Philosophy** means a 'love of Wisdom', and as this new movement began to develop, the Gods found themselves challenged by this new enquiry into knowledge and thought.

The Sophists (meaning the Wise) were a group of philosophers who held the decidedly dangerous view that 'Truth' was relative to each man, and that it was pointless to search for the *'absolute truth as regards nature and morals'*. Statements such as this upset not only the Gods, but also the Eupatrids, who began to feel the ground moving under their feet in a *disturbing* way! But although the Sophists loved wisdom, they loved survival even more, and so when things began to get a little rough for them, they bowed their heads to the State – in order to escape execution.

With the Sophists we first get the phrase, "When in Athens do as the Athenians do", which was them corrupted by the Romans to be known as, "When in Rome do as the Romans do." But whichever city you prefer to quote in this saying, the message is quite plain, and really means, "Don't rock the boat!"

As **Protagoras,** a leading Sophist, said (in order to excuse himself and manage to sit on the fence with both crowds at once) "About the Gods, I cannot know that they exist or that they do not exist; the obscurity of these matters and the shortness of human life are impediments to such knowledge". And with this short statement Protagoras managed to save his intellectual credibility, and his hide!

One is forced to admire Protagoras, because quite obviously he would have made a marvellous 20th Century Minister of Economics, as he had that special political talent for saying both 'yes' and 'no' at the same time, and *meaning neither particle of speech!* (Protagoras may have been dead these many years, but his spirit lives on in practically every modern government in the world.)

So the Sophists survived this period of Persecutions of Heretics, by being extremely sophisticated (or wise) while less skilful men (like Socrates) went down before the rising tide of fascism.

Socrates of course, had made the mistake of discovering that Man had a *Soul* – or at least Socrates *thought* that Man had one! And he compounded this mistake, by declaring it publicly and, tearing around Athens, engaging people in talk; and pestering the merchants (who just wanted to get on with the job of making money) by posing them uncomfortable questions about their way of life!

The political rulers of Athens however, decided that he should go. And Socrates was therefore advised to drink the hemlock – and be done with his philosophical problems forever.

It was quite obvious to the Rulers, that if ordinary men had souls, then this would put them almost on a par with the Gods; and if people started thinking that they were as good as the Gods; then sooner, or later, they would start thinking they were as good *as the Eupatrids as well!*

These Eupatrids of the "Golden Age" were not only extremely powerful, and extremely jealous of their position, but were as big a bunch of hypocrites, as you could hope to meet in a month of Sundays. The God System and the Family System were nothing more than a gigantic cover for their legalised illegalities. All the Athenians of wealth and influence liked wearing the mask of respectability and pretending that they were good 'Temple Goers', and that their wives and families were sacred to them; while at the same time, the only 'Temples' they really worshipped in, were their own 'Counting Houses'. And their wives and families were left securely locked away at home (with all the other valuables) while *they* were indulging themselves, in all sorts of forbidden, and exotic fruit! The exotic fruit were generally the 'Hetaera', the companions, or women of pleasure, who were the only really, exciting females around Athens. As most, if not all the Eupatrid marriages were 'arranged', the men were extremely bored with their cow-like wives (who were all rather like Hera of Olympus) and so, they, the men, sought to emulate Zeus, and spent their time gadding around.

There was never any shortage of **'Hetaera'** either, because the Greeks were always bringing back foreign women, as part of the 'loot', from their foreign expeditions and wars. Even Pericles himself was 'living in sin', with one of these glamourous ladies, who went by the name of Aspasia, of Miletus.

This was truly the period when Athens had reached such heights of political importance (after defeating the Persians) and such a degree of wealth (partly from commerce, and partly from war reparations paid by the Persians) that she was the 'Mother City of the World, and the Mother of the Gods!' Although Virgil, later attributed this characteristic to Rome, in order to apease a certain expansionist and irascible Roman Emperor, by the name of Augustus.

So into this extremely hypocritical, affluent, unhappy, and expansionist Athenian society of the 5th Century B.C. the Dionysos cult erupted, with all the forceful impact of the Hippie Movement of the 1960s in the U.S.A.

This cult included such activities as drinking oneself into a state of intoxication, so that one could have a mystical experience, or in other words – be as drunk as a God!

The movement also involved physical tests; the taking of drugs; and, attempts at a mystic union with this God who could bring the assurance of Everlasting Life. And besides the Dionysos cult there were other cults (including that pertaining to Demeter as well as the Orphic and Pythagorean Cults) which sprang up at this time; attempting to supplement, rather than to replace, the conventional religion of the State. But gradually however these Cults began to assume more importance in the minds of the people, and things looked bad for the Olympians!

There was a popular return to Nature, with worshipping in the woods rather than in city temples; and the followers of Dionysos took off their clothes; and frenzied with wine; ran screaming through the trees; tearing to pieces, wild creatures in their path, and, devouring them.

In fact one can say, that with the Cult of Dionysos, there was something for everyone. That is for Nudists; Nature Lovers; Hippies; and Alcoholics. The only possible exception being the wild creatures, who did not find this movement particularly pleasant, as it involved the disturbance of their natural habitat!

135

Many wild women (possibly unemployed Hetaera) also took to the woods in pursuit of this new cult, and they were known as the 'Maenads' or the 'Bacchantes'. They lived on herbs and berries, and the milk of wild goats; slept in the grass; and ran around – altogether rather like the Flower Children of the 20th Century A.D.!

There were also some rather nasty incidents reported, such as the slaying of people, when emotions were high from drink, or drugs; and this God of Life, Death, and Resurrection, became such a powerful fixation in the minds of people, that he almost threatened to overturn, the now elderly Olympian Gods.

This God of Wine was both kind and cruel, and many different stories grew up about him. Some of them were possibly copied from myths regarding other foreign deities, like Aton in Egypt, who had also preferred the freedom of nature, to the temples and building of the city.

Most remarkable of all however, is the appeal Dionysos had for women; who seemed to have a greater admiration for him and his grapes, than did the men! There is a story concerning him in Thebes (where Dionysos supposedly originated from) which illustrates this point quite well.

Dionysos, accompanied by the **'Maenads'**, went to Thebes to establish his wine drinking movement there. But Pentheus, the king of Thebes, didn't recognise him. (Semele, Dionysos' mother had in fact been the Aunt of **Pentheus**.)

Maybe of course, Pentheus *did* recognise his cousin, and thought that he was returning to claim some family property by right of his dead mother. But what ever the truth of the matter, Pentheus thoroughly *disliked* and *disapproved* of Dionysos, and had him thrown in prison, along with his band of Maenads!

The 'Maenads' flew forth from the prison, as the locks could not hold them; and they took off for the woods to begin singing and drinking once more. For some reason or other, the locks on the prison holding Dionysos did not give so easily, so he stayed there on his own, in his cold cell, probably working out a good year for a table claret.

Reclining Maenad: by Titian

Pentheus sent the soldiers to bring Dionysos forth for questioning, but afterwards he wished he hadn't, because he found the prisoner's replies to be both senseless, and, insulting.

After a period of nonsensical dialogue between them, Dionysos said with calm assurance, which made Pentheus see red, "You cannot imprison me, for God will set me free!"

"God?" jeered Pentheus.

"Yes," replied Dionysos. "God is here, and he sees my suffering. He is where I am, and you cannot see him, for you are not pure!" (This seems a rather brazen statement for a wine-drinker to make to a tee-totaller, but then Dionysos was never one to pull his punches!)

"I see no God"! said Pentheus with a sneer, and ordered the soldiers to remove the vile, wine smelling tramp, and to put him back in his prison.

"The wrongs you do me, are wrongs done to the Gods!" warned Dionysos. And just to prove his point, he flew the coop that night; and escaped to the woods outside Thebes; with half the women of the town, in tow. Even the mother and sisters of Pentheus went to join the dance, and succeeded in drinking themselves insensible.

"In Vino Veritas" it is said, and perhaps it is true; for when Pentheus came after his mother and sisters (to try and persuade them to come on home, and get the fire started, and put the kettle on to boil) they saw him, not, as the Revered Male Leader of their family; but as a rangy, mountain lion. And they sprang on him – tore him limb from limb – and drank his blood!

Having disposed of this venerable member of their clan, the Late Pentheus' mother and sisters then sobered up, and grew remorseful. But it was too late by then; as it always is; and as people always realise on the *'morning'* after, the *'night before'!*

This story, and others of the same ilk, helped prove that Dionysos was both the benefactor and the destroyer of Man. And that he could bring Man happiness or tragedy as alcohol is both a stimulant, and a depressant.

People drank up Dionysos, and got him inside their skins; thus becoming immortal for a short time; before mortal like, they regurgitated the God again, or excreted his influence from their chemical make-up, in some other way. Drink gave people 'Dutch Courage' for all types of conflicts, and under its influence they became *temporarily Divine!*

So in the 5th Century, the Delphi Wine Festival to Dionysos was specifically encouraged by the 'Establishment' in Ancient Greece, and for several days, the people were entitled to complete abandoned enjoyment. The Demeter Festivals were not so condoned, and were secret, select, ceremonies, about which it was forbidden to write. But Dionysos on the contrary, was smiled on, and even *pushed* to the people. "If you can't beat 'em, join 'em!" the Olympian Gods, and the Eupatrids said pragmatically. "It's better to have a bit of drunkeness rather than a Revolution!"

This Festival of Wine celebrating Dionysos was held in Spring, and no other business was conducted at this time of National Holiday, and no one was even put in prison during this time. In fact, prisoners were actually pardoned, and freed, and allowed to join the people in the theatres who gathered to watch plays being performed about Dionysos, and the other Gods.

The **Dionysos Festival** therefore led indirectly, or directly, to the rise in Drama; and to the Birth of Tragedy, and Comedy.

Dionysos was a figure of Tragedy, because like Persephone, he died every year in the winter, torn to pieces by the Titans, or, in some other stories, by Hera's orders. But he always rose to life again, to be the joyful God of Resurrection, as well as the God of Suffering. Dionysos proved Socrates' personal theory that there was a 'Soul', and that this 'Soul' would live on forever – even if the body died! This was the same theory behind the worship of **Aton** in Egypt, and **Zoroastrianism** in Persia; and it was the theory that Socrates would eventually be executed for propounding. Of course there were other people also going on about Souls but we don't have time to cover them all, and anyway, *Souls'* (like Bank Accounts) are personal things, and no one is really interested in anyone else's, except his own!

Anyhow, this was the Resurrection Cult, which was first sketched in myth form with the story of Persephone, but which later became developed and defined by the story and character of Dionysos. Unlike Persephone, Dionysos did not actually live in the Underworld, but he visited it; managed to steal away his mother from Death; and therefore showed the invincibility of Man – because Dionysos was half Man as well as half God. He was naturally the perfect combination of all the elements necessary to make an enduring myth!

During the 5th Century, as the Dionysos Cult grew (and

139

Drama expanded from its base of being simply a form o
Religious Festivities) many theatres were built – and the peopl
were encouraged to attend this form of amusement, which wa
also a clever part of the State Propaganda Machinery. As th
theatres were free, most people did indeed attend and the Stat
Plan for indoctrination worked like a dream!

The Dramas which emerged, began from the word **'Tragedy'**
which actually means, the 'Song of the Goat'. This stems fron
the fact that in the Religious Rites, Dionysos was generall
connected with an accompanying band of Satyrs.

These Satyrs were zoomorphic creatures (half men and hal
goats) and during the wine festivals, men representing then
dressed in goat skins, and sang, and danced, and eventuall
began to speak lines of plays specially written for Dionysos; an
gradually this led to a new art form, and the creation of grea
Tragedies on other themes.

So the world received for the first time, the works o
Aeschylus, Sophocles, and Euripides; and the Epidauro
Theatre in Athens was specially built to accommodate this nev
art form.

Wine can therefore be said to have given birth to Drama, tc
thought,to tears; and eventually, to laughter; because finall
Comedy was also born, with the plays of **Aristophanes,** a maste
satirist on politics, and the mores of the Athenians of his day

Although the **Parthenon** had been built at great expense anc
effort (the effort being made by the builders themselves, and th
slaves!) in a desperate attempt to keep the Old Olympian Gods i
their position of importance in the minds of the populace, th
new Cults became increasingly more important, and popular.

The Gods of *Justice, Order* and *Beauty,* found themselve
being replaced, by a couple of Vegetation Deities, whc
represented *Bread,* and *Wine.* And this behaviour of the peopl
was not only frightening, it was downright insulting!

But the Olympians should have realised that Bread and Win
are essentials that will *never* go out of fashion, and in fac

Dionysos and Demeter are as necessary today, as they were two and a half thousand years ago. Doubtless in another two and a half thousand years people will still be worshipping them.

Eat, Drink, and Be Merry, is a Universal Creed, and the only point on which all Mankind can agree – irrespective of nationality, economics, or class! And besides the physical aspects of these Deities, the Metaphysical sides to their characters are even more appealing. The idea of resurrection after death is generally attractive to practically every one; as no one really welcomes the thought of a 'permanent end of the road'. Furthermore if the Mediterranean world hadn't turned Christian when it did, it seems sure that Dionysos and Demeter would have taken over the place. With all due respect, it can be said that there's a lot of 'Christ' in Dionysos, or at least in the characteristics attributed to him. Anyhow, the original Dionysos Cult as practised by the peasants, had a lot in common, with the ideas of early Christianity, and could be said to have "paved the way" to the Christian Religion. If people couldn't find their resurrection one way, then they turned towards another, and hence the Christian population grew. Therefore, next time you see an empty wine bottle, treat it with care – after all it is the dwelling place of a God, and Dionysos was the spirit indirectly responsible for the whole Western civilization of today!

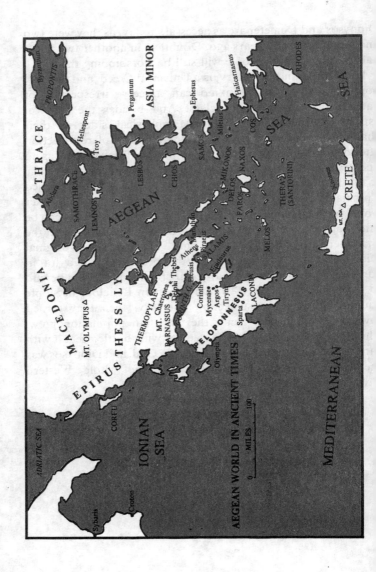

AEGEAN WORLD IN ANCIENT TIMES

CHAPTER VII

THE QUEST OF THE GOLDEN FLEECE

The original story first came to light by way of **Apollonius of Rhodes;** a Greek poet in the Third Century. The 'Quest' concerns the exploits of **Jason** and the **Argonauts,** and is supposed to have taken place a generation earlier than the **Odyssey.** This is also the story of **Medea** and Jason, and their personal tragedy. Both **Pindar** the Poet, and **Euripides** the tragedian writer of the Fifth Century, have supplied many basic elements of this version of the myth – however, all sarcastic comments, and touches of levity, are entirely the fault of the writer of this Guide!

The tale begins with the Greek King **Athamas,** who, like many other men, became tired of his wife. Unlike other men however, he decided *to do* something about this marital fatigue. Therefore, after ditching **Nephele** (his first wife) he took a second wife called Ino; the daughter of **Cadmus,** King of Thebes.

Nephele was worried in case this second wife (Ino) might try to kill her (Nephele's) two children **Helles** and **Phrixus,** and as the story proves she was quite right to be worried, as that is *exactly* what happened!

Ino determined to have the boy, Phrixus, sacrificed, on account of the failure of the corn harvest. *But, the only reason that the corn harvest failed, was because Ino, had caused it to fail, in the first place!*

Although she wasn't a great admirer of other people's children, Ino had a diabolically clever mind, because she went to a great deal of trouble destroying the seed *before* it was even planted; and then, she bribed someone to announce that the '*Oracle*' had disclosed, that the *only way* to avert famine, was, to *KILL OFF YOUNG PHRIXUS!*

King Athamas (after a slight interval of blowing his nose and wiping his eyes) consented fairly amicably to this suggestion, so it may be understood that he didn't particularly care for his son anymore than did Ino the wicked step-mother.

But lo and behold! Just as Phrixus was lying stretched out on the altar stone, and the priests were sharpening up their knives, along came Hermes – who had been sent in answer to the prayers of Nephele, to save her son from death.

Hermes did not come alone, but accompanied by a magnificent ram, which had a fleece of pure gold; and onto the back of this ram, Phrixus and his sister Helle were placed, in order to fly off into the deep blue yonder.

While the trio were soaring over the strait of water between Europe and Asia, Phrixus let his sister Helle fall and drown; and this place then became known as the **Hellespont,** or Sea of Helle. (Allowing his sister to drown in this way, seems totally irresponsible, and leads one to suppose that Phrixus was a thoroughly horrible brat, who didn't deserve to be saved in the first place!)

After ridding himself of his sister (mythology is full of similar examples of fraternal fidelity!) Phrixus and the ram finally came to land in the country of the **Colchis,** on the 'Unfriendly', or 'Black Sea'.

Now young Phrixus should by rights have been killed by these people, as they loathed and detested *All Greeks!* but although young, he had already learnt how to make a political deal, as shrewdly as anyone older, and wiser than he.

He decided simply to cut the ram's throat (which seems an odd way to repay an animal which has just saved your life) and to present the fleece to King **Aetes** of Colchis, in return for political asylum, and the hand of one of his daughters in marriage. He wasn't very particular about which hand, or which daughter – the main motive being – to get a new passport!

This saga now leaves Phrixus wheeling and dealing in Colchis, and returns to Greece, where we find some more of his relations in trouble, with various people usurping their lands and titles.

This mis-used member of Phrixus' careless clan, was a king,

whose kingdom had been taken from him by a man called **Pelias** (who also happened to be his nephew) so we see that this is really a Palace Revolution or Family Squabble (and isn't every Palace Revolution simply a Family Squabble?) which will waste a lot of good Peasant blood and good harvesting time, before it is finished.

The deposed king in this case, happened to have a son called Jason, and the Reader may finally relax with a sigh of relief, because we have at last got to the main theme of the story!

One bright morning, Jason came trotting into the Palace of Pelias, and facing him eyeball to eyeball, demanded that he (Jason) have his father's throne restored to him.

Pelias beamed most agreeably and replied, "But of course, my dear boy! There's just a small formality to be gone through first."

Then wiley old Pelias spun Jason a yarn about how the ghost of Phrixus was haunting him at night, requesting to have the Golden Fleece brought back to Greece from Colchis, and how he, Pelias, was desperate to accomplish this; but how he didn't have the courage, or the knowledge, to begin this quest himself.

He praised Jason for his fine athletic build, and said how he realised that going on dangerous adventures was something every young man hoped to do, and wanted to do, and even, *needed to do!* (and more rubbish of this sort) until Jason was salivering in desperation to throw himself into glorious battle.

(It seems obvious that Jason was a pretty stupid and impetuous youth – but then aren't they all! If the young *weren't* so stupid, then they'd have the sense to stay at home enjoying themselves, instead of running off to foreign lands to fight the wars of old men (who naturally hate and fear their *own country's youth,* far more than they loathe *their enemy!)*

Hera of Olympus now decided to float down and fill the minds of all these silly young men with dreams of glory; thus demonstrating the typical female and maternal desire to sacrifice their young to the State, and to destroy them in senseless bloody

145

battles. Losing a son in war often provides a good 'coffee-morning' talking point for a great many women, and makes a change from discussing their difficult pregnancies and their neighbours' husbands' infidelities.

A boat was found (the 'Argo') and the 'Nauts' or sailors were assembled. Provisions were collected. And everything was prepared for the quest to begin.

The crew of the **'Argo'**, i.e. the 'Argonauts', were a motly group, which included: – **Hercules,** a strong man and Hero; **Orpheus,** a musician; Castor, and his inseparable brother **Pollux; Achilles'** father, **Peleus;** and others.

None of this crowd had an iota of sense between them, and Pelias rubbed his hands with glee as he saw them leaving the port, and felt sure that he'd *never* be troubled by Jason again!

The first island which the adventurers came to was Lemnos, which had just witnessed the birth of the Women's Liberation Movement, and where all the females had taken charge, after murdering all the men! (The only exception being the old king, who had been mercifully exempted from execution and then set adrift on a raft in the sea, and left to die naturally and slowly, from thirst and sun-stroke!)

However, having at last freed themselves from the tyranny of men, these progressive women seemed to have begun to regret it (or maybe their self-enforced sexual starvation just proved too great!) because from the moment that they saw Jason and the Argonauts coming into port, they gladly surrendered all their homes and their hearts to this influx of male tourists.

Jason and company therefore thoroughly enjoyed themselves in Lemnos – apart from one small disaster, which occurred just prior to their leaving.

Hylas, the armour – bearer of Hercules, got himself somewhat entangled with a water nymph, who drew him down into the drink, and wouldn't let him return to the ship. At least this is how mythology describes the incident, but it is probably far more accurate to state that he got embroiled with a 'bar girl'; and lost

146

Hercules slaying *Hydra*

the ship by oversleeping, on the morning of its departure.

Hercules was left behind in Lemnos also, because *he* went off in search of his 'buddie', and never returned to the ship either! (Sailors have been doing the same thing ever since, as far as one can determine from Hollywood movies.)

After dallying with the damsels of Lemnos, the ship put in at the island of the **'Harpies',** who were frightful flying creatures (probably bats) with hooked beaks and claws, and who always left a terrible smell behind them whenever they vacated a place.

The original and rightful inhabitant of this island, was an old man called Phineus, who had the gift of Prophecy, and who, by being so talented, had enraged **Zeus,** who hated any mortal knowing the future, before, He, Zeus, had worked it out for himself!

It was in fact Zeus, who had sent the Harpies to swoop down and excrete all over the food everytime poor old Phineus tried to eat. The result of this punishment being that Phineus, had grown extremely thin, and was falling to pieces from the enforced dietary regime.

The Argonauts hated to see a man deprived of his dinner in this way as they were all hearty eaters themselves, so the Sons of Boreas, the North Wind, decided to kill off the Harpies, the next time they flew down to attack Phineus' smorgasbord.

Accordingly, Phineus got the table ready; the Harpies appeared in the sky; and just as the arrows were quivering in the bows; Iris, the Messenger of the Rainbow, flew down, and instructed them to stop.

"I am hereby notified to inform you," she said, shimmering in the air above their heads, "that the Harpies are the Hounds of Zeus, and therefore must *not be killed!* I am also authorised to tell you that Zeus is now sorry that he allowed Phineus to starve for so long, but due to the "Secrecy Act", and "Information Regarding the Security of the State", He felt it in the best interests of everyone, that Phineus should not be opening his big mouth and telling people things they shouldn't know!

Especially", she continued, settling herself more comfortably on a cloud, *"especially* those matters concerning the private life of Zeus Himself, which He would not like to have divulged to *all and sundry!"*

"All right!" said Phineus. "I understand! He doesn't want me to tell Hera where he is, or what he's up to, or with whom!"

"That's exactly!" replied Iris, smiling radiantly. "I'm glad to see that you caught my drift so quickly!" And without so much as a by your leave, or a cheerio, she shimmered off; leaving them to eat their meal in peace.

In gratitude to the Argonauts for preserving for him the culinary pleasures of life, Phineus explained to them how to pass through the dangerous Clashing Rocks or 'Symplegades', which lay on their way to Colchis.

Next day, having followed the old man's advice to a 'T', they manged to stay afloat, and finally arrived within the 'Three-Mile-Limit' of the land of the **Amazons.**

Surprisingly enough, the Amazons were the daughters of that peace loving nymph, **Harmony.** Their father however, had been **Ares,** the God of War, and the girls tended to take after their paternal parent in their attitude to life.

Jason and his crew (ever mindful of their experiences in Lemnos) hurried past without so much as casting a glance in the direction of these Lady Warriors, as they felt that they really couldn't give themselves over entirely, to the continual satisfaction of sexually frustrated women!

With noble brows fixed firmly forward, they streered past the Caucasus (where Prometheus was still being eaten, daily, by the eagle on the rocks) and arrived at Colchis. Here, they berthed the boat, and set about having a wash and brush-up before dinner.

Up in Olympus there was great consternation, because Hera, having originally pushed all the Argonauts to go; *now,* didn't know what to do with them! She felt, that without intervention, on *someone's* part, the whole expedition might end in disaster! So, to her surprise, as well as Aphrodite's, she begged the

149

Amazone on horseback from the temple of Asclepios at Epidaurus

Goddess of Love to leave off painting her toe-nails, and to do something to help these valiant Greek sailors.

Aphrodite was so bemused by the sight of a suppliant Step-Mother, that she consented; and calling Eros from the garden, where he had been happily uprooting all Zeus' prize rose bushes; she promised him a beautiful new ball to play with, if he would run down to Colchis and shoot one of his arrows into Medea's heart.

As Medea, the daughter of King **Aetes** of Colchis, was skilled in sorcery, she could be of great assistance to Jason-if only she were foolish enough to fall in love with him, and therefore decide to help him!

And so it happened, as the Gods had ordained!

Jason and his men entered the court of **King Aetes,** where Medea saw Jason, and immediately fell in love! (A disastrous thing for her, and quite out of character too, as she was a highly intelligent woman, and Jason was only a clumsy, sports-mad, oaf!)

Here we have a prime example of Love being Blind!

King Aetes invited the Greeks to make themselves at home, and to bathe and to eat, because he was an hospitable man (as were most people in those days, when the opportunities for social life were rather lacking; and when a foreign face to stare at for a few hours, proved a suitable divertissement!)

Jason, who had no head for tact and diplomacy, announced immediately that they were seeking the Golden Fleece; and that they wanted to take it back to Grece; *and that if* King Aetes wanted some payment for this piece of wool; then they would perform any feat of daring which he might like to set before them!

Then King Actes (who was a fairly crafty man himself) decided to tell Jason a Cock and Bull story about how in his youth, *he,* had managed to plough a field with two bulls whose feet were made of bronze, and whose collective breath were flames of fire; and how, having ploughed the field, he'd sown the

151

teeth of a dragon in it (for want of anything better being available at the time) and how a crop of armed men had sprung up, who had to be cut down as they advanced. And all this, *he* (King Aetes) wanted *him* (Jason) to do again for him, King Aetes, to watch – *as a sort of a trip down memory lane!*

Jason, the idiot, swallowed the lot; and not very happy (like Ares he was actually a secret coward!) but resigned to his Fate; he set off to tackle these gory tasks; and Medea knew she'd have her work cut out to save him from killing himself right at the start!

Firstly, Medea supplied Jason with an ointment which made his body invulnerable to all attacks on it. Then she helped him with the Bulls, and the **Dragon's Teeth,** and even told him how to get rid of the crop of armed men who sprang up in the field.

However, **Aetes** wasn't going to give up the Fleece so easily. Therefore Medea took the Argonauts to the place where it was kept and guarded by a really vicious serpent, and she lulled the reptile to sleep with a song, so that Jason could finally *win his quest.*

Despite all these endeavours on the part of Medea, Aetes sent his son to kill Jason, and this is when Medea made her fatal (the first in a long line of same) mistake. She sided with the braggard Jason; slew her own brother; and thereby earned a *very bad reputation* for herself in mythology! But it really wasn't her fault, because that old cow Hera, had forced Medea into this unfortunate action, by causing her to fall in love with Jason in the first place!

Having gotten Medea to dispose of all the opposition, Jason and his merry men set off for Greece, taking both the Fleece and Medea with them. Jason had told Medea (when she realised what a horrendous thing she had done by killing her brother) "If you will come to Greece with us, you will be worshipped for what you have done for us, and you and I, will *never be parted — except in death!"*

This statement must have been one of the greatest lies first recorded in history, and all War Brides should read the story of the Golden Fleece, in order to have a really good idea about how base and faithless a man can be, and about how unhappy they may become – when once they have left their native land far behind them.

Madame Butterfly also discovered the same thing, a few years later – with an *American* sailor! But it doesn't seem to matter what nationality it is. It's just in the general nature of men (and *sailors in particular)* to be false to women!

On the way back to Piraeus, the ship stopped in Crete, where Medea saved everyone from certain death, by destroying the bronze monster, the Talus, who lived there. This Talus was invincible, apart from his ankle (shades of Achilles coming into this story) and Medea summoned up the hounds of Hades, to bite him at this weak point in his anatomy, and to send him running off like a London Postman from a pack of corgis!

Back in Greece, Jason discovered his family in a complete shambles, as **Pelias** had forced Jason's father (an obviously weak-minded man) to kill himself; and Jason's mother had then died (supposedly) from grief!

Medea took care of Pelias for Jason, as he, mighty warrior that he was, didn't want to dirty his hands or his consicience with murder; and she ingeniously managed to contrive that *Pelias' daughters* should remove their old man from this life of pain and suffering.

What she did, was to visit Pelias' daughters in the kitchen of the palace, and to show them a really smart Colchisian receipe for reconstituting, or re-cycling, old rams.

The directions for this receipe involved the cutting up of an ancient sheep, putting it into a cooking pot, and snapping the fingers; whereupon they presto! out would come a frisky, young, baby lamb, alive and kicking!

Pelia's daughters were extremely dumb (the sort that Door-to-Door Salesmen love!) and they thought that it would be a marvellous way to make their father young again. So, they cut their Daddy up in little pieces, threw in a handful of spices, and then turned to Medea for further instructions on how to proceed – *only to find that she'd gone off and left them without the final details on how to re-assemble dear Pappa!*

Once the problem with Pelias was finally out of the way, Jason and Medea settled down in Corinth, where Medea gave birth to two fine sons, and you might have thought that everything in the garden was lovely – *BUT,* Jason fell victim to the old Greek Dowry system, and decided that he was *tired of Medea.*

Now the King of Corinth had a daughter, and the King of Corinth was very rich, *and the King of Corinth promised Jason a suitable sum of money to take his daughter off his hands!*

And as Medea had run out of money, and we may suppose that she was showing her age (after all, excitement and assassinations tend to wear badly on members of the female sex) so Jason resolved to leave her and the boys, and to marry a younger, and richer, *GREEK* woman.

Medea accused Jason of infidelity, and he replied nonchalantly, "What can I do?" and rolled his eys towards Olympus.

The King of Corinth then declared that Medea' must be banished, and once, more Jason sighed helplessly, "What can I do?" and this time rolled his eyes towards **Hades.**

Then Medea decided that she'd go down fighting; so she killed Jason's bride-to-be (before the nuptials could take place) and then turned her attentions to considering the fate of herself and her children.

Realising that the Greeks would either kill her sons, or even worse, enslave them (and life as a slave was infinitely worse than death in those days, and possibly in our days as well!) Medea decided to kill them herself, in a quick, and painless way.

It will not have escaped the Reader's critical eye, that the writer is in full accord with Medea on this point and that she feels that Medea has been unjustly condemned in history as a bad mother, when in actual fact she was only trying to protect her

Asembly of Gods and Heroes

children by removing them from the scene – albeit permanently!
She was, in point of fact, a stirring example of the *Motherly
Protective Instinct* at work!

Just after this gristly deed was done, Jason turned up to
complain to Medea about her ruining his business arrangements,
by killing off his rich Corinthian goose with the golden egg.
Unfortunately for Jason, he arrived only in time to see his
estranged wife tripping off (the Gods knew where, and they
weren't telling!) in a chariot, drawn by a couple of fiery dragons.

There is only one small point in this story which still worries
me, and that is; *if* Medea had this chariot ready and waiting, *why
didn't she take her children with her in it?*

Still and all, nobody's perfect, and children quite obviously
weren't very popular with their parents in those days; and any
children reading this fable, should be glad they were born in the
enlightened Twentieth Century, when it is not *so* easy, to dispose
of unwanted, and unloved progeny!

CHAPTER VIII

THE ILIAD

The original story of the Iliad is by Homer – or various poets, whose collective works were *assembled* under the *name of Homer.*

There are many different aspects of this story concerning the destruction of Ilium (Troy) and its inhabitants. These various aspects have been described by the well-known writers of Greek Tragedy:– Aeschylus, Euripides, and Sophocles; also by **Apollodorus,** a writer from the Fifth Century; and by that great Cis-alpine Celt of the Roman Empire, **Virgil.** The version below is a type of conglomerate of all these writers' works – a Russian Salad Iliad.

The city of Troy, existed approximately one thousand and two hundred years before the birth of Christ, and was situated at Ilium at the Eastern end of the Mediterranean Sea. This place was originally known as the **Hellespont,** where Helle, the sister of Phrixus was drowned in the story of the Quest for the Golden Fleece. Ilium, is today, an area of Turkey.

The Trojan War (according to Greek Mythology) was caused by the Gods themselves, who, due to a disagreement in Olympus, decided that the issue at stake, should be fought out by their 'proxies' – the Greeks, and, the Trojans.

Historians however, have asserted that the Trojan War was caused by the Greeks desire to capture Troy, as it was an important port and strategic area which would control the 'Graniary Centres' of the Middle East, and grain was badly needed by the Greeks at this time in their evolution as a rapidly growing young empire.

The Greeks, at this stage in their history, were only beginning to expand, and they could be likened to an–ever hungry adolescent, continually on the rampage in the kitchen. Troy, and its inhabitants, due to their close proximity to the wheat and corn supplies, were regarded by the Greeks simply as a packet of biscuits, to be wolfed down between school, and a game of tennis.

Any tiny twinge of guilt which the Greeks might have felt about the destruction of Troy, they assuaged quite easily and quite rapidly also, by blaming the entire catastrophe on the Gods!

Besides destroying the entire civilization, the culture of Ilium (which at that time was obviously superior to the culture of Greece) was usurped, along with the Gods of Troy – who deserted their Trojan devotees, and went happily off with the victorious Greeks. But as Brennus the Celtic leader said at a later period in history to an unhappy and defeated Roman soldier in 387 B.C. "Vae victis!" ("Woe to the conquered!") He might equally have remarked that the Gods go with the winners – *every time!!*

History, however, is wonderfully just, and whatever suffering the Greeks caused the Trojans, and whatever Gods they stole from them – they paid for, at a later stage, when the Romans marched in, and swiped *all* the Olympian Deities – *and a good deal more besides!* The wheels of Justice may grind slowly, but they do grind exceedingly small!

As mythology explains in this story, the Gods of Olympus turned against the Trojans, and sided with the Greeks. By reading between the lines, we may detect the real meaning to be that the 'Gods' or the 'Fates' turned from Troy to Greece, and that as the Greeks emerged triumphant from this war, so the older civilizations and older cultures, and even the older homes of the Gods, moved into the Greek world.

Gods always go where they can live most successfully and luxuriously, and that means that they go to the richest, and most successful, and most *powerful* nation! In the Chapter devoted to the Gods in the Twentieth Century, we will see that the Greek

Gods of Olympus have changed their passports many times since Athens fell to the Romans in the Second Century B.C.

Anyway, here is the story of the Iliad, according to Greek mythology.

Up in Olympus, there was held the first Beauty Contest in the history of Men and Gods, and like all Beauty Contests there was great acrimony, bribery, and corruption, caused by it.

One is rather surprised to learn that liberated female Goddesses would bother to stoop to humiliate themselves, by asking an ordinary mortal male, to judge them in this matter; but, that is what they did . This story definitely proves the theory, that the *Gods themselves* are terribly insecure; and possibly, *have need of the mortals, more, than the mortals, have need of them!*

Anyway, this contest was between Hera, Aphrodite, and Athena (Artemis, showed great sense in not bothering with such rubbish!) and they turned Olympus into a veritable shambles in order to appease their petty, and ridiculous vanities.

The trouble began when the evil Goddess of Discord, **"Eris"** *wasn't* invited to a wedding banquet in Olympus, as the Gods *never* liked to see her around the place, and thought to avoid any nasty scenes by simply leaving her name off the Guest List.

Eris was furious with this treatment from the Olympians, and revenged herself by quietly gate-crashing this 'shin-dig', and by throwing through the window of the Palace, a golden apple marked, "For the Fairest".

Naturally, the three principal Goddesses tried to pick it up; and naturally they came to blows, and tore each other's hair out, and ripped each other's diaphanous gowns in competition; so that Zeus was finally forced to intervene.

But Zeus and the other male Gods in Olympus, were too canny to get involved in this dispute, as they well knew that "Hell hath no fury like a Woman scorned!" so they 'passed the buck' to the Earthlings.

"Down in Troy," said Zeus, "lives a man called **Paris,** who is the greatest judge of female beauty in the world. In fact, *that,* is about the *only* subject he is qualified to discourse on, as he has *never* put his mind to doing *anything,* other than, *running around after women!* Go down and ask him to choose between you, because he has much more experience in these matters than I."

Thus, Zeus extricated himself from this sticky diplomatic situation, and poor profligate Paris, was presented with the challenge which was to bring about not only his own downfall, but the downfall of his people as well!

Paris, was the son of the King of Troy and as he had never shown much acumen for affairs of State (or indeed for affairs of any kind, bar those which involved the Female Gender) he was in disgrace.

Because of his great propensity for chasing after a well rounded pair of heels, his father had sent him off to train as a shepherd, in the hope that he would learn something useful to help himself in later life (and from which he could possibly derive a living, or source of income.)

King **Priam** had decided that any sort of profession or trade, was better than none; and that Paris was much better away from the Court of **Ilium,** where he only caused scandals, and upset political alliances, in his pursuit of passion.

Therefore, at the start of the story, Paris is to be found, sitting under a tree in a field, and watching his girl-friend, **Oenone,** a shepherdess, rounding up the sheep for him.

(All physical activity (outside of that in the bed-room) was terribly tiring for Paris; and he felt that any work which *Oenone did,* was amply repaid by his caresses in the evening, after she had cooked his supper, and finished washing his socks! Paris was *not* a believer in the Protestant Work Ethos.)

Into this idyllic scene stepped the three Goddesses, who tossed the apple to Paris, and immediately demanded that he make his choice. In order to help him along (and clear his mind as it were) they all offered him a type of incentive bonus if he would choose *'correctly'*.

Hera promised to make Paris, the Lord of Europe and Asia, if only he would choose her. And she advised him to do so rapidly, as she didn't have much time to fool around!

As being Lord of Europe and Asia, sounded like extraordinarily hard work to Paris, he wasn't particularly impressed with the size of her bribe. He knew from experience in his father's Court, that you couldn't enjoy the Pleasures of State, without enduring the Headaches as well!   Athena than said that if he chose her, she would see to it that Paris led the Trojans to victory over the Greeks, and that he would leave Greece in ruins – *obliterated from the map!*

Paris however was quite appalled at the idea, because he had always had a distaste for the physical rigours of battle, and was a strong advocate of the "Make Love – Not War" principle.

Aphrodite, the only Goddess of the three, who understood the psychology of Paris, then said that *if* he would choose *her,* as the most fair of the Goddesses in Olympus; then she would *personally see to it that the really Fairest Woman* in the world, *would be his!*

By 'Fairest', the meaning in those days, was *not only* the most beautiful, but also the *whitest* in skin colouring, because sun-tanned beauties were *not in vogue* in Ancient Greece or Troy. To have a brown skin in those days meant that one was a peasant and worked in the fields, as the *Aristocrats, never,* ventured out in the hot sun, to destroy their lilly-white epidermis, and bring about skin cancer to mar their anatomy. (If the Olympians were to come down and see the bathing Beauties on the beaches of Crete nowdays, they would probably all have heart attacks from culture shock!)

As Paris was a sensualist of the highest order (with no desire nor interest in either Power, or, Riches) he found no difficulty in making his choice, and immediately gave the **Golden Apple of Discord** to Aphrodite, and thereby awarded her the title of **'Fairest Goddess** of Olympus."

The Contenders

In all fairness to Paris, it must be stated that probably Aphrodite was miles ahead of the other two in the 'looks department' anyway. After all, most of the poets describe Hera as vaguely resembling a 'cow', and Athena (in her helmet and shield) was hardly the picture of lyrical femininity; more like a 'butch motor-cyclist!'

But, the 'Judgement of Paris' had been passed. Oenone, was forgotten in a trice. And Paris left immediately with Aphrodite, to find the ravishing Helen of Sparta, whose name, 'Helene', is derived from the ancient Greek word, **'Selene'**, meaning the 'White Moon'.

Hera and Athena likewise only stayed long enough, to tell pitiful Oenone that she'd better find herself another man, before they too departed – in order to conspire together, and to bring mischief to Paris, and his native city, Troy.

Meanwhile in Olympus, Zeus sighed to himself with relief (and with smug satisfaction) that he had been rescued from a dangerous situation, and that, He, the Captain of the Gods, was still *shrewder* than any good-looking young Trojan stallion!

"Lust is all very well," said Zeus to himself, "but it must be kept in its *proper perspective!* Everything in moderation! That's *My* motto!" And so saying, he flew off to rendevous with a sweet young nymph in Egypt, while Hera was busy occupying herself with thoughts of revenge on the Trojans.

Paris and Aphrodite meanwhile, were still journeying towards Sparta, and the Fair **Helen,** who was in fact, the daughter of Zeus and **Leda.**

This Leda, was the Spartan Queen, who had developed a passion for Swans. And strange as that may seem, it was at least *preferable* to being enamoured of a *Bull,* as **Pasiphae** (the wife of King Minos of Crete) had been! However, time is short, and duty calls, and the interesting perversions of the early inhabitants of Crete, must be undertaken in *another book;* because we cannot leave Helen dangling in mid-air, so to speak.

Relatively speaking, Helen was also the sister of **Clytemnestra,** and the sister of Castor and Pollux (of the Argonauts) and her father was *reputed* to be King **Tyndareus** of Crete-although *everyone knew* that it was *really Zeus!*

Poor old Tyndareus suffered all his married life from his wife's infidelity, and was a continual source of amusement for his subjects; who knew full well that he was a prize Cuckold, and that all his children had been born on the wrong side of the bed. It makes one wonder if this 'cuckolding' of the King of Sparta might have been one of the factors contributing to the fierce, aggressive, dispositions of the Spartans, and to their rigid, puritanical life in general. Most fascistic states generally seem to have some type of sexual hang-up!

Helen, sought after by many, had finally been married off to **Menelaus** (the brother of **Agamemnon**) who was then made the new *King of Sparta,* so that as well as winning the most beautiful woman in the world, he had also acquired a *powerful kingdom!*

Helen's father Tyndareus, then attempted to unify the Greek States, by telling all the suitors (or, by this time, *ex-suitors* of Helen) that they should fight for the honour of Helen's husband (Menelaus) should anyone *attempt* to spirit *Helen anyway from him!* The "face that sank a thousand ships" was really being used as a symbol of unity, and of the Greek Idea-in order to bring everyone under the Spartan command, and to eventually expand the Greek Empire of City-States!

In other words, *Sparta* was the *chief state* in the Greek world at this time during the **Mycenaean** period and there was a type of unity (albeit short lived) among the Greeks, and which was directed *against* the Trojans, whom they envied, and sought to conquer and to dispossess!

But the fair Helen was dreadfully unhappy in Sparta, and who can blame her? As some Athenian wit reported of Sparta in those days, "The Spartans live such dreary lives, that it is no wonder they are happy to go to their deaths so readily!"

Everyone perpetually marched around Sparta in a continual state of war-preparedness, and Spartan mothers continually told their sons to "Come home on your shield, or don't bother to come home at all!" (Pacifists were *not* thought highly of!)

Therefore, when Paris showed up, Helen was only *too* happy to leave Sparta, and go with him to Troy. And the Greeks (especially the Spartans) were only *too* happy to have the excuse to go to war! It is after all quite senseless having an Arms Race, if you never *get a chance to use the Arms!*

No sooner had the Lovers' ship begun to disappear on the horizon, than the Greeks started rooting out their spears, and buckling on their belts, and shouting to their wives to cut them some sandwiches to eat on the way to battle.

But the Greeks had a problem, and it was THIS. Their two most famous warriors, **Odysseus,** King of the island of Ithaca; and **Achilles** the son of **Peleus,** and the sea nymph Thetis – *didn't WANT to go to battle!*

Odysseus and Achilles were both sensible men, who realising that they hadn't started this stupid war in the first place, and as they didn't believe in it, then decided that they weren't going to become involved in it.

Therefore, they both decided to resist the 'Call-up', and as the World's first 'Draft-Dodgers', each thought up novel ways to preserve his own peace and property.

Odysseus pretended to have gone mad, and when the army messenger came to Ithaca to present him his draft papers, he found him ploughing in the fields – sowing the furrows with salt – instead of seed.

But the messenger was also a crafty person, and he didn't believe that Odysseus was as mad as he wished to appear, so, he grabbed the young son of Odysseus, and put *him* in the path of the plough.

Odysseus stopped ploughing at once (rather than run over his son and heir) and the messenger, smirking broadly, handed him his orders to appear for battle. Odysseus had no choice therefore but to agree.

Meanwhile, Achilles was helped, in *his* dilemma, by his mother Thetis, who being a sea nymph, knew that her son would suffer a mortal blow, if he went to this war. Therefore, she sent him to live in the Court of a Palace, in another City (and dressed him up as a woman) in order to escape detection form the authorities.

Unfortunately for Achilles, he was caught with his pants down, and a petticoat on, and shipped out to Troy – just as he was beginning to enjoy himself as a *transvestite!*

Before the Greek Fleet actually set sail from Aulis, the Commander in Chief, Agamemnon, decided to appease Poseidon and the other water Gods by sacrificing to them. He also thought it might be a good way of stirring up a little patriotism in his men, who seemed decidedly squeamish about the whole venture!

Unlike we enlightened people of the Twentieth Century, he did not choose to swing a *bottle of champagne* over the prow (indeed, the Ancient Greeks didn't go in for such luxuries anyway!) but instead, to cut the jugular vein of a *young virgin* (his daughter, Iphigenia, incidentally) and to allow *her blood,* to bless the departure of the Fleet, and to speed them on their way!

He very cunningly persuaded **Iphigenia** to come to **Aulis,** by sending her a message that he had arranged a marriage for her, with Achilles, and when she arrived at the altar dressed in all her finery, he quickly summoned the priests, to come and slit her pretty throat!

In the Mythology there is some ridiculous story about how the Greeks were *forced* to sacrifice this way to **Poseidon,** because, He (Poseidon) was angry with the *Greeks,* because *Artemis* was angry with the *Greeks,* becuse *some of them had been killing mother rabbits and their baby bunnies!*

This is quite obviously a bold-faced lie, because, *Poseidon,* was *never* known to be overly fond of **Artemis;** and besides this,

Artemis, would never have ordered the death of a *young virgin girl* (it was much more likely to have been a young man!) because *Artemis* was a bit of *a Man-Hater!* (The whole story is completely out of character for Artemis anyway, and I don't know what Homer was thinking of when he wrote it!) if in fact he did!

The real reason for the sacrifice is more likely to have been that the Greeks *just didn't want to go off to war!* Because in those days, wars took even *longer* than they do now! And the majority of men, had no desire to absent themselves, and to leave their wives and property *to be used or destroyed by others,* while their backs were turned!

So Agamemnon decided to kill his own daughter Iphigenia, as a sign, that *if he, were willing,* to spill the blood of his family, then everyone else, *should be willing,* to do likewise!!

This Agamemnon of the House of **Atreus,** was a thorough sod, and he caused untold misery to countless people, including his wife Clytemnestra, and his younger daughter **Electra,** – among others!

There is yet another story, that Artemis saved the life of Iphigenia, and sent her off to live with the **Taurians,** on the **Crimea.** But this is more than likely an attempt at white-washing the monstrous behaviour of the Greeks,and in particular, the behaviour of Agamemnon who was a *great* Greek Hero and much admired (although not much of a family man by all accounts!)

Anyhow, from the moment that the Greeks landed in Troy, all they did was to argue and fight among themselves; rape all the Trojan women; and loot whatever they could find. (And as they'd had to have a virgin slaughtered, in order to get them there in the first place, one must say one is not really surprised!!)

Achilles and Agamemnon in particular, did *nothing else,* but steal women and booty from each other, and in general behaved so outrageously, that one wonders *why* Mythology is ever allowed to sully the innocence of the average school-child by being taught to him in the classroom. (Perhaps however, the

Achilles retiring from the fray.

average school-child of today, is not as innocent, as we might like to think!)

Indeed, that many faceted God, Apollo, became so incensed with rage at the Greeks' behaviour, that he sent down the sun, to drive them mad with heat, and to burn them up! While **Thetis,** the mother of Achilles, appeared to her son, and ordered him to be done with the Greeks, and to leave their camp at once. In fact, *all* the Gods in Olympus, were disturbed with what they saw happening down below, and *even Hera* and *Athena,* began to pretend that they'd never heard the work 'Greek' before, and started brushing up their rather rusty Trojan in case it should be necessary.

We can in fact, *definitely* say and with *certainly,* that *at this stage,* in the proceedings of the Trojan War, things were *Not going well, for the Greeks!*

Most of the Gods had by now, begun to side with the Trojans, especially Aphrodite, and because of her-Ares (who always followed the dictates of the Goddess of Love, so that Love and War were inseparably bound together!)

Likewise, Apollo favoured the Trojans, because he fancied **Hector,** the Hero of Troy; and Artemis, sided with her twin brother on this subject, as she did on all others.

Zeus himself thought that the Trojans were infinitely superior to the Greeks, but he preferred to look impartial; although Poseidon, threw in his trident on the side of the Greeks, because they were sailors, and the Trojans weren't.

Hera and Athena, the scorned losers of the Beauty Contest, were naturally, Anti-Trojan-Pro-Greek-and PLOTTING!!

Zeus then decided to send a false dream to Agamemnon, depicting him beating the Trojans to a pulp, and Agamemnon (who knew the price of everything, and the value of nothing) believed it, and fool-hardily went into battle, *without* Achilles (who had retired from the fray–due more to a disagreement over the distribution of captured women, than to the remonstrances of his mother!)

The Greek Army without Achilles, was like a hot dog without the sausage, and so, was *completely slaughtered* by the Trojans; who chased the tattered remnants, bruised and bleeding, back into camp!

Then **Menelaus** and Paris had a small 'contre temps', which was interrupted continually by Aphrodite, who kept rescuing Paris, any time the blows of battle came too near.

Menelaus got as mad as all get out, to see Paris being picked up by Aphrodite every time he swung out at him; and even the Trojans accused Paris of cowardice, and told him to stop hiding behind a woman's skirts, and to come out and fight like a man!

Needless to relate, Paris refused.

By now the Trojans had become thoroughly fed-up with the whole issue of Helen and Paris, and decided to give Helen back to the Greeks and to end the whole shooting-mess.

"What do we want with another female in the country? We've already got too many, if you ask me!" they muttered. "Give her back to her husband, for Gods' sake' (any Gods!) and be done with it!"

But Hera and Athena, wanted to see the Trojans completely destroyed, and had no intention of allowing this war to end so abruptly and humanely. Therefore they tied up their skirts, and flew down to land a few blows for themselves, and thereby start things up again on the battle field.

On the Greek Side, **Ajax** (well-known for his capacity to clean sinks) and **Diomedes** (unknown for anything, due to his unfortunately long name, which has no commercial appeal!) leapt out into the field, and began to take on everyone in sight.

They viciously beat up any Trojan on whom they could manage to lay their hands, and even Hector, as well as Aeneas (the son of Aphrodite) were roughed up by them.

Aphrodite came down from Olympus, to pick up **Aeneas,** who was lying sadly battered on the ground; but Diomedes jumped up and shouted at her so loudly, that she dropped her son in shock, and retreated crying, and confused, to Olympus.

Zeus laughed at Aphrodite, and said she'd better stick to Love
– Making, and not concern herself with War, but Apollo went
down, rescued Aeneas, and carried him off to **Pergamos,** a holy
place of healing in Troy, from where (after a suitable period of
recuperation) he returned to join the front line once more.

Diomedes continued tearing the Trojans limb from limb, so
that Ares (cowering under his bed in Olympus) was forced to go
down and fight alongside the Trojans, in order to try and help
them to win. The Trojans themselves, were not actually all that
glad to see Ares (as he was a *lousy fighter!*) but as they couldn't
do much to stop him, they just had to accept the situation!

Upon seeing Ares taking off for Troy, Hera and Athena
decided to go down again as well, and leapt about, screaming
and catawauling like a bunch of banshees, and completely
destroying *everyone's* concentration, *on either side!*

The First Lady of Olympus shouted encouragingly to the
Greek Army, "You can kill that lousy, no good – good for –
nothing son of mine, and I'll be grateful! Don't mind me, and the
fact that I'm his mother! Why, that cur has never given me a
day's happiness since he was first conceived, and I'm *damned* if I
want to see him around my house any longer! Filling up his room
with spears, and javelins, and other types of rubbish! Coming in
and going out, at all hours! Never so much as a thank you, or a
by your leave. Just poke him in the eye with that stick there,
Athena dear, and let's be done with the rascal, for once and all!"

So Athena obligingly threw a spear at Ares. "Break your
mother's heart, would you?" And Ares took off, yelping with
pain and fear, like a dog who suddenly finds himself sitting on an
ant nest.

Half the warriors on the battle-field nearly died with fright
themselves, at the sound which Ares made; but they picked
themselves up, manfully, and continued – because they had no
other appointments for the day, and nowhere else to go anyway!

Up in Olympus, Ares blubbered to Zeus and asked him to stop
Athena from interrupting his games, but Zeus only roared in

Hera and Athena taking on Ares at Ilium. "Break your Mother's heart, would you?"

disgust, and told him to take his hang-dog face out of His Presence.

"You *always* side with her! It's not fair! You never care about anyone except your favourite Athena!" Ares sobbed, blowing his immortal nose.

"Why, you lilly-livered, snivelling coward! Of course I side with her! The only decent child I ever had, and a great source of comfort to me in my old age! You, on the other hand, remind me of *your mother!* And the whole world knows how much I've suffered at the hands of *that woman!* Get out of my sight, before I take to you myself!" And Zeus boxed Ares over the head, and sent him howling back to his bedroom.

Down in Troy, meanwhile, Hector's mother had offered Athena a beautiful new gown, if only she *would stop the fight.* As Athena was not the most fashion conscious of the Goddesses, and spent most of her life in working clothes anyway, the bribe was not accepted, and the battle went on.

On account of his bitter dislike for his wife, Zeus also decided to fly down to Troy for the day, and in order to spite Hera, he joined the Trojan Army, and pretty soon, things began to turn in their favour. Especially as Achilles was still brooding in his tent about the women which Agamemnon had stolen from him, and the Greeks (without Achilles) were never known to be particularly successful.

Realising that she would have to do a bit of skull-duggery, if she were to save the day for the Greeks, Hera flew up to Olympus; broke and entered into Aphrodite's room; stole the Love Goddess' girdle of Enchantment; and having slung it around her preponderous girth, appeared, smiling bewitchingly, to stand before the Captain of the Gods.

With the magic girdle lending her a seductiveness and beauty hitherto unknown, Hera beguiled Zeus into leaving the battle field for a short siesta in his bed chamber, and during his absence naturally enough, the Trojans began to LOSE!

Too late, Zeus realised his mistake, and cast Hera from him! But down below, it was almost over for the inhabitants of Ilium, and as Hector, the main combattant for the Trojans, had been grieviously wounded, so **Iris** (the **Rainbow Goddess**) was despatched, to send a message to Poseidon to stop assisting the Greeks. This was of little avail however, because Achilles had decided to re-join the Greek trenches once more, due to his friend **Patroclus** having been killed by Hector (before Hector himself, began to bite the dust!)

Then Achilles, in magical armour, and assisted by Athena (who was fetching and carrying his spears for him) stood proudly erect, ready to face the Trojan Hero Hector, for the final round.

(Actually it wasn't much good his standing erect to face poor Hector, because he, Hector, was busy grovelling on the ground, and wishing that he'd never gotten out of bed that morning, because he'd had a really disastrous day and all due, so he thought, to his not having followed his Bio-Rhythm Chart!)

Poor Hector never stood a chance, and when he finally did manage to get up and try to take a swing at Achilles, Athena was there at the back of him, the whole time, pulling his hair, and breathing garlic down the front of his neck.

Around about this time, all the Gods in Olympus started attacking each other as well, with Hera blacking the eyes of Artemis, and Poseidon spitting salt water at Apollo. Only Zeus (due to his age and position) managed to keep his sacred body inviolate, and refrained from these physical excesses.

Hector fell (released at last from having to make a fool of himself in the cause of heroism) and the rest of the Greek Army took over, and chopped, and pulled, and twisted his body, and generally enjoyed themselves, hacking him to pieces. And just as they were getting ready to feed him to their dogs, Zeus intervened, and said, "enough is enough" and that they should think about Pluto down in Hades, and the trouble he had identifying and classifying badly mangled bodies. So the Greeks handed back the body of Hector for burial, and after the required mourning period of nine days–they all got ready to massacre each other again.

Achilles now became drunk with power, and took to trotting up and down on the fields of Ilium, beating his chest, and hollering like Tarzan, and being altogether *too cocky* for his own good.

He had forgotten (if indeed he had ever known it in the first place!) that when his mother had dipped him in the **River Styx** when he was a baby, in order to immunize him against all the ravages of life (plus mumps, measles, and whooping cough) she had been talking to some other women, and consequently neglected to douse his left ankle properly.

This oversight on the part of Thetis, was to cost Achilles his life; and proves the point that women should *never* gossip when they're washing the baby – because good gossip needs a lot of attention – and a baby just gets in the way!

This incident in the 'Iliad' is also supposed to prove that *everyone* in life has a weak point or other, but we all knew that anyway! And most of us have *more* than one weak point to begin with anyhow!

So, as Achilles was marching around being thoroughly objectionable; Paris came slyly out from behind a rock where he had been hiding, and with the help of Apollo, fired an arrow directly into the Greek's heel.

Achilles died. And by his removal from the scene, created even greater dismay and argument among his comrades, who took to fighting with each other as *to whom,* his armour (and his women) should go!

One cannot help but admire the Greeks and their survival instinct; for here in the midst of death and disease, they took to worrying over who should inherit what, and how to make the most out of Achilles' slender Estate.

Finally Odysseus got the arms, but Ajax felt hard-done-by and resentful, so he got drunk and attacked the sheep which the

Greeks had brought along, to feed them during their long years of battle.

Having cut the throats of all the animals, he suddenly gave into a fit of remorse (upon sobering-up and realising that he'd mistaken the poor dumb animals for the Greek Army) and filled with both guilt and fury, he slashed his own throat as well, and hastened on his way to Hades.

Then the Greeks killed Paris, who – on his death bed – suddenly remembered the shepherdess, Oenone, whom he had left behind, and he begged to be returned to her bosom, in order that her love might save him.

But Oenone cried, "Me! Help that slob! Never! I'd sooner see him die!"

And so he did. And then she too became remorseful, like Ajax, and killed herself; and Pluto down in Hades had an arbitration dispute with **Charon,** because with all the dying that was going on, the **Ferryman** never got to have a lunch break any more, and was in consequence demanding 'Time and a Half', or else a 'Go Slow' Strike, to press his point.

The Greek Army then turned to thievery in order to beat the Trojans to their knees, and removed the sacred image of Pallas Athena from where it stood in the **Palladium** in Ilium.

But even this was to no avail, and still the City Walls remained impregnable. So, they were forced to turn their thoughts to more inventive things, and finally, the **'Wooden Horse',** was born!

Having hidden most of the army in the caves around the bay (and a good few soldiers inside the 'Horse' itself) the Greeks then pretended to leave Troy, and sailed out of the harbour, leaving a spy, called Sinon, behind them.

Sinon (an out of work actor from Athens) had been well primed to tell a shaggy dog story to the Trojans about how sorry they (the Greeks) had become, on realising, how much they'd been distressing the entire population of Ilium these ten years.

"The Greeks," said **Sinon,** "are truly sorry for all the ruckus they have caused, and as an act of contrition and reparation, they are leaving for you, the People of Troy, this magnificent Wooden Horse, which you may remove forthwith into the temple of Athena, so that she will bless your city, and protect you forever!"

"Hold on there!" cried Laocoon, the High Priest of Troy. "I don't believe a word of it! The Greeks are a remarkably stingy people, and we *all* know *that!* Why would they be wanting to give anything away if it were really any good?"

But everbody else shouted, "Shame! Shame! How can you look a Gift Horse in the mouth?" and such like rubbish; and Poseidon raced up from the beach, with a sea serpent; grabbed up **Laocoon** and his two sons; and deposited them out in the **Adriatic,** where nobody could hear them and their warnings any more.

Then **Cassandra,** King Priam's daughter, appeared on the edge of the Temple steps, and shouted dire warnings and curses. But *nobody* listened to her *either!*

"Alright! Alright then! Go your own ways, and you will see! I've been prophesizing without pay for years, and still you damn idiots never listen to me! Woe to the whole lot of you! I've done my best! And when the trouble starts, I'll think you not to come screaming to me, to come and save you!" and she exited to the Temple, while her father shook his head, and her mother whispered to a friend of hers, "That's the worst of educating your daughters. They always become so self-opinionated and aggressive!"

So the Horse stayed in the City; and in the night, the Greeks came out of it; opened the city gates to the rest of their men; and attacked all the Trojans as they lay sleeping in their beds.

The Greek Army really enjoyed themselves in Ilium that night, and raped, and burnt and looted, and threw *all* the children down from the City Walls! And any women that they'd happened to miss out on killing, they took back to Greece as slaves and concubines.

Laocoon and his sons

All the Gods in Olympus became horrified at this scene of carnage, and hid their faces and wept, but none of them stirred a finger to help the Trojans. All that is except Aphrodite, who ran up and down as ineffectually as The International Red Cross, but *still managed* to help a few Trojans to escape – including her son **Aeneas,** who, according to **Virgil,** in his long poem of the same name, would one day be the Founder of Rome.

So Troy fell, and the Gods became Greek completely, and felt no shame at deserting the mortals who had once praised them. For after all, as Zeus, might have said, "A God *has to make a living!* And looking at the state of the economy in Troy, there really wasn't any reason for a God to stay around. The Trojans obviously could not afford us any more, and so we really *had to go.* Life among the Greeks is *not so bad.* And the way they're building up their empire, why, we'll soon be *richer than before!"*

CHAPTER IX

THE ODYSSEY

After the destruction of Troy, the Gods of Olympus (who had hitherto been helping the Greeks) suddenly turned against them; and, like a bunch of contradictory and obstinate cows, gave them all sorts of trouble. At least that is the story according to Homer (and according to **Euripides,** in his play, **"The Trojan Women".**)

"The Odyssey" by **Homer,** concerns the adventures and wanderings of a certain Captain Odysseus, who, on leaving Troy, after the battle which lasted ten years, spent *another ten years* – trying to get home to his wife and son!

It could be, one supposes, that **Odysseus** was actually just a hopeless navigator, or even possibly, that he liked looking at the world a little, before he settled down on his farm again. Soldiers always find difficulty in re-adjusting to Peace-Time conditions. As the post World War II song said, 'How ye gona get them down on farm, after they've seen Paree?"

However, according to the Greeks, these wanderings and misadventures of Odysseus', were all caused by the Gods. And naturally it's much more comfortable to have someone else to blame for all the troubles in the world, rather than simply to see it as a result of *our own stupidity, and contrariness!*

So we return to the devastation of Troy, with the City on fire, the babies being slung down from the cliffs, and the women being rounded up to be taken home to Greece as 'Household-Helps' of some capacity or other.

While the Greeks were tearing through the place, plundering, murdering and looting, Cassandra (the Prophetess to whom nobody had listened) was clinging to the curtains in the Temple, and praying that everyone would go home, so that she could get a little rest!

Some rowdy Greek soldiers came storming into this sanctuary, and dragged Cassandra off in order to pleasure themselves with her, and thereby brought down upon their heads, the curses of the great God Apollo (who had secretly been an ardent admirer of hers!)

This love-affair of Apollo's had been a rather one-sided affair, as Cassandra had not returned his affection; which was why he had cursed her, and seen to it that nobody ever *looked at,* let alone *listened to her,* every time she prophesized; and this action of Apollo's had really broken Cassandra's heart, as there is absolutely no use in being a prophet (or prophetess) if no one ever pays attention to you!

Apollo might have been a little peeved about this case of unrequited love, *but,* when he saw those rough and ungainly mortals enjoying themselves with the woman *he loved,* he *became mad with rage,* and decided to expend all his not inconsiderable (and celestial) energy, in revenging this sacrilege.

Even Athena, to whom he went to grouch and complain, agreed with him and said, "Why, I'm a virgin myself, and if Cassandra wanted to stay that way, then she had every right! Besides which, she just happened to be holding on to an image of myself when they came into the temple and pulled her out, and I don't take kindly to that sort of behaviour. It gives a Goddess a bad name, when a devotee is attacked in the midst of the devotion!" The Goddess of Education then straightened her helmet in a purposeful manner, which boded ill for somebody in the world. "It is absolutely disgusting, and I think now that I backed the wrong horse in this affair. The Greeks are an impossible people to deal with, and I shall see to it that they pay for what they've done!"

So saying, Athena sailed off to have a word with Poseidon, who agreed to stir the waters up, and to give the Greeks a few things to think about on their way home.

The result, of all this action on Poseidon's part, was that most of the ships leaving Troy were wrecked, and countless lives were lost. Unfortunately half these lost lives happened to be Trojan women, who had been put aboard as slaves bound for Greece. But then, when the Gods are angry, *everyone* had better look out, because *Justice* always seems to strike down the *innocent* – along with the *guilty!*

There was of course, one other point which made the Gods so angry with the Greeks; and that was, that the Greeks, it seems, had forgotten the Gods; and took to thinking that *they'd* destroyed Troy all by themselves; and in their plunder, they'd neglected to award the Gods, *Their fair share of the loot!* (Self-interest is always a great motivator of both Gods and Men!)

As their employees had ceased to give satisfaction, as it were, the Gods decided to swamp the lot, and send them down below.

(Cassandra, incidentally, who was being taken back to Greece by Agamemnon, was spared the fate of drowning; – only to be stabbed to death, by Agamemnon's wife, who didn't appreciate her husband bringing home a foreign 'au pair' girl, to help her in the house!)

Odysseus likewise, was also saved from drowning in the storms which raged the **Aegean** coast. But back on the island of Ithaca, his wife **Penelope,** and his son Telemachus, were having a hard time trying to keep the family estate together, while waiting for their Lord and Master's return.

As soon as the news of the disaster at sea had reached **Ithaca,** the house of Odysseus became full of suitors, who came to inspect the property (and the *wife!*) and who took it for granted that Penelope would now be in great need of a new man, in order to manage her affairs.

These suitors were hardly sensitive, retiring creatures, but coarse, and vulgar opportunists, who sat around the kitchen all day long, drinking tea; telling dirty stories; and getting in everyone's way! This short of thing might have been endurable for a week or two, but this lot cluttered up the place for nigh on ten years, and Penelope and Telemachus thought they'd go mad with the strain.

The Suitors even brought their own priests – to marry themselves to Penelope; and a poet or two – to engage in light verse, in order to better fill in the time. And when they'd done with the tea, they started on the wine; and the corridors rang with the sounds of bawdy songs, and flowed, with the remnants of over-turned tankards.

The servants all left, one by one (as they couldn't abide trying to mop under prone, drunken, bodies.) And the cooks gave up even *attempting* to feed such gargantuan appetites. And Telemachus sat sulking in the cellars, and reading books on how to develop his muscles.

"Enough is enough!" said Penelope one day, unconsciously echoing the words of Zeus at Ilium. "I can stand this crowd no longer!"

Then Athena (who had always had a soft spot for Odysseus, and had always taken a great interest in his family) came down, took a quick look round, and agreed that life in Ithaca had become quite insupportable, and that something must be done to put an end to these dowry hunting slobs.

Telemachus was eventually persuaded to come up from the cellar, and to leave his bicep building alone; and to go to find Nestor, or Menelaus (the husband of Helen, formerly of Troy, and now back home in Sparta) and to see what news either of them might have, regarding Odysseus, and where he could be found.

So Telemachus set off for Sparta, and the home of Menelaus and Helen, where things seemed to have improved tremendously, for Homer describes the Hall of Menelaus' house as being a residence of "blazing splendour".

Perhaps, the rich Spartans were not as Spartan as they would have us believe. Or perhaps, Menelaus had decided to give the 'Fair Helen' all the home comforts which she could desire; in order to *KEEP* her at home – and stop her running off with other men!

Or perhaps, the house was full of 'booty' from the seige of Troy. *Or perhaps* (and this is probably the *real reason)* **Telemachus** was so used to seeing a house of dirty drunks, and broken furniture, that any other place which was a little clean, might have *seemed* to be a place of 'blazing splendour', to his eyes!

Helen herself, seemed to be quietly happy, and reconciled to domestic life in Sparta. (One imagines that the achievement of having "sunk a thousand ships", would have proved a suitably satisfying enough experience *to last one for a Life-Time!)*

Filling her time by doing the dishes, and beating the servants, might have sometimes seemed tame to her (after what she had been through) but no one could have accused her of *not having contributed something to the world!*

The night Telemachus arrived, Menelaus got to talking about the war (as all old soldiers are prone to do) and about all his adventures while coming home, especially of when he had been washed up on an Egyptian island called **'Pharos',** and of the problems that he had faced there.

"It was a sea nymph who helped me out of that place," said Menelaus, "and without her help, I'd still be there, to this day." And he sighed with such nostalgia, that the company in the room took to fingering their goblets in discomfort, and Helen rose and began re-arranging the shades.

"Ah yes! I remember her well!" and he sighed again, and more lustily, so that everyone there wished to hell that he'd remember that he was a married man, and would keep his sexual reminiscences to himself!

"Such a *pretty little thing!"* he continued. "You know, those Egyptian nymphs are really *something!* It's the way they move their wings!

"I do believe *my dear,* that Telemachus is more interested in his father, rather than in hearing about your sociological studies of the Egyptian Female Lower Deities!" Helen said with straightened lips, and shot Menelaus a look which boded him ill in the bedroom that night. (It will be noted by the Reader that both Helen, and Athena, had this ability for 'boding people ill' their eyes!)

"Yes! My father! What of him?" Telemachus leaned forward, and flexed a muscle, just to fill his time; and thought how dumb the older generation were; and wondered what an Egyptian nymph could ever have seen in Menelaus, in the first place!

"Hump! Well! This nymph," (and Menelaus stole an upward glance at Helen, and began to wish that he'd kept his big mouth shut) "this nymph, as I was saying, told me how to get off that island, by catching a sea god called Proteus, who could, and did, supply me with all the information I needed to return to Sparta, and to my *DARLING WIFE!*" (And Menelaus looked at Helen *again*. To see if he had gained his absolution!)

"But what has that to do with Dad?" Telemachus said, wishing these aging idiots would stop shooting each other pregnant glances.

"Well, this sea god **Proteus** also gave me word of your father," Menelaus said. "And he told me that Odysseus was captive on the island of the nymph **Calypso,** where he had been for many years, and may possibly stay for many more to come!" And Menelaus wiped away a tear, which might have sprung from either *sorrow,* or, *envy!*

"But what does *she want* with *my father?*" Telemachus interjected. "Why doesn't she let him go?"

"Ah! These nymphs! You wouldn't understand! A boy of your age – how could you understand?" Menelaus replied. "Love sick they are! And crazy with passion! Just waiting for a strong Greek man to come by, to warm them in the night!"

"But my father's already got a wife and family! Why doesn't he tell her that, and come on home?"

"Oh, he did! He certainly did! We all do, er, did. I mean, er, none of us *wants to stay!*" And Menelaus hung his head, and in his confusion kicked the dog beneath the table; and was immediately bitten!

"What my husband is trying to say," hissed Helen, bending forward, and knocking Menelaus in the solar plexus with her elbow, "is that your father, unlike *some men* we could *name"* her voice took on an ominous tone at this statement, "is *true* to his marriage vows, and refuses to satisfy the *wanton demands* of that trollop Calypso! Which is why she holds him on her island, and refuses to let him go, until *he gives in to her desires!*

"On the beach, there he sits!" Menelaus' eyes had a far-away gaze. "Searching the horizon every day. Thinking of home and his loved ones. And praying for deliverance from this red-blooded woman!"

And Menelaus sighed again, and noisily blew his nose, and completely ignored Helen and the fury that was radiating from her, and which was enough to ignite a fire, and roast a fair-sized hog.

"Things haven't been the same since those days!" Menelaus began to sob, and weep openly into his cups. "Wars and women! That's what this world's about! Oh! *If only I were young again!"*

Then everybody wept, and shouted "Wars and Women!" and fell on the floor in emotion; and Telemachus retired to bed to wonder why he'd ever bothered to read the history of the Heroes, when quite obviously these men were only drunken sots, and not at all the types to light the fire of imagination and idealism in the young.

"I only hope my father's not as bad as that!" he muttered to himself, and fell into the slumber of the young – secure and sonorous.

Up in Olympus, a general meeting was called by Athena (who favoured Odysseus) and she declared, that something must be done for the valiant sea captain to aid his return; and now that Poseidon (who definitely *didn't* favour Odysseus) was away feasting in **Ethiopia,** it was as good a time as any, to secure the release of Odysseus from Calypso's island, and to bring him home.

Zeus agreed, and despatched Hermes on his sandals of imperishable – 24 carat gold (which proved how wealthy Hermes was, and why it was correct that he should have been chosen to be the God of Commerce!) and with his left hand clutching the wand which could charm men's eyes to slumber, he flew down to find Calypso, and to tell her the bad news.

"Well, this is the last straw!" said Calypso. "And who does Zeus think he is? Just because I'm a nymph and a woman, he thinks he can push me around! He's a despot and a bully! And anyway," she added, "I don't have any ships, or crew of sailors at my command, and *how am I to get that wretched pansy off my island!*"

(It must be noted that Calypso would not ordinarily have spoken so uncautiously, but years of pursuing a man who threw her sex-appeal back in her face, had made her ego suffer, and consequently caused her personality to undergo a change.

"That of course is *your* business, *not* mine. I simply give the messages around the place, and ranting and raving at me, won't get you anywhere!" Hermes retorted. And having delivered his usual bad tidings. he smiled and headed off.

"Well, if that isn't the darndest thing!" said Calypso, and shouted to Odysseus to come and see her, and that she was setting him free.

But Odysseus refused to believe her, and hid sulking in a cave, thinking that she wanted to drown him instead.

(If, in point of fact, Calypso *had decided* to drown Odysseus, who could *blame* her? *After all,* if it is *true* that Odysseus never once gave into her wiles in all those ten years, then *presumably,* Calypso was *tremendously frustrated,* and would, likely as not, have been *justified* in *murdering this man* who had so *disregarded his duty to Woman-Hood!*)

Finally however, Odysseus was convinced that Calypso was really intent on seeing him gone, as she herself set about getting rid of him in no uncertain manner, so he crept out of his cave in order to enjoy the spectacle of her labour.

Firstly Calypso helped him to cut down twenty large trees, in order to make a raft (one can't help wondering why Odysseus had never thought of doing this for himself, in all the time he'd had at his disposal, and considering all the trees there were in the place!) and then she filled up the raft with all the delicacies she could wangle out of the nearest Mediterranean P.X., and threw her reluctant Greek Lover in, on top of them.

So Odysseus set sail, and for seventeen days, he coasted along very nicely, until one morning when he was espied by Poseidon who was finally returning from his lengthy vacation in Ethiopia.

"Why, that no good Odysseus is free again! They let him go while my back was turned! I'll show him you can't teach an old sea dog new tricks!" and so saying, Poseidon sent all the winds of the north, south, east and west, to dance across the sea, and send the raft off course.

So the raft spun round and up and down, and Odysseus hung on desperately, throwing-up breakfast, lunch, and dinner until he was eventually rescued from his predicament by the kindly Goddess Ino of the Slim Ankles.

This **Ino,** we know better from the story of "Jason and the **Golden Fleece,**" as a wicked queen who tried to diabolically destroy her step-children, and in truth could not (by any stretch of the imagination) be described as 'kindly'!

But it appears that Homer was what in modern jargon we might call a 'leg man', and that the sight of a prettily turned ankle sent him all aquiver. So he therefore assigned to Ino a kindly and sympathetic character – and one– more in fitting with her physique!

As the "Odyssey" by Homer, was written *before* the "Quest of the Golden Fleece" by **Apollodorus,** we can safely assume that Ino really *was* a kindly Goddess, but that *Apollodorus* (for some reason best known to himself) decided that *he didn't like her,* and *that is why her character was changed to that of a coldly, calculatingly, evil and mercenary woman!*

The real problem however, is that *although* the "Quest" is an *older story in time, it was written at a later date* than the "Odyssey". So how is one to know for *sure,* which pen portrait is correct?

(Please Note! The above, is a prime example of the old conundrum, "Which comes first? The Chicken, or the Egg?")

Anyhow, in the "Odyssey", Ino is ⌐ good soul who rises like a sea-gull from the briney blue, and directs Odysseus on how to save his life, by diving from the raft, and swimming for the shore.

So Odysseus swam for two days and two nights without ceasing (which goes to show what a stout fellow he was) and Poseidon, eventually got tired of watching him struggle in the waves, and went off to stir up trouble somewhere else.

Then Athena stepped in and calmed down the waves for her favourite mortal, and Odysseus was at last able to swim to an island, dig himself a hole in the sand, and sleep 'till morning.'

In the morning, who should arrive at the beach to do the family washing, but Princess **Nausicaa,** whose father was the King of the **Phaeacians** – the country in which Odysseus now found himself.

The Phaeacians were a kind and worthy people, and not known to greatly lack for money, but strangely enough, the washing of the Royal Linen was a type of hobby for their young princess. (As she was still unmarried, who knows but perhaps her family thought that the sight of her doing something really useful, might stir some young man up to propose to marry her – thereby taking her off her family's hands!)

Nausicaa and her maids had their own special way of doing things however, because they used to load up the family donkey-cart with the dirty clothing; take it to a river which flowed near the sea; throw the linen in the water; and dance up and down on it until it was clean.

After this they used to strip off their own clothes; cover their bodies with olive oil (in order to produce an even tan) and play around in the sun until it was time to return home.

Odysseus holding out on Calypso. "I'm a poor man but I'm virtuous!"

In the midst of their revelry that particular morning, they suddenly saw a gaunt, naked, man approaching them, and all (apart from Nausica) ran off screaming hysterically like well brought-up virgins should on such occasions!

The Princess however, showed greater composure (possibly having had greater experience in facing naked men before) and stood her ground, and asked Odysseus what it was he wanted, and why, undressed as he was, he was wandering around in her country?

"If it's selling door-to-door, you are, you'll not be welcome in this town! And your only customers are likely to be the dogs!" said Nausicaa, spiritedly.

Then Odysseus turned on all the blarney, and told her that he thought she was some sort of divinity, and that he hoped, that, *as she was some type of Goddess,* she would help him in his great distress.

Nausicaa, naturally enough, was thrilled to be thought of as a Goddess, and decided to take Odysseus home to her parents. *But,* very wisely, she decided *to clothe him* before taking him there.

Also, she thought it would be better for all concerned, if she *went on ahead,* and he followed behind. *Because* (as she explained) she had her *'reputation'* to think of, and *unmarried* girls couldn't be seen walking the countryside with *strange men* — even those wearing clothes!

Furthermore, she told him, that when he entered the palace, he should go *straight* to her mother, the *Queen,* to beg political asylum, because whatever it was that the *Queen elected to do,* the King would readily agree to, and *follow.*

Odysseus adhered closely to all Nausicaa's commandments, and that night, was a safe and honoured guest in the palace, happily ensconsed in the best chair, with a glass of something strong in front of him, and telling his tale to the King and Chiefs of Phaeacia, in return for their lavish hospitality.

The Story which Odysseus told the Phaeacians

After leaving Troy, and undergoing the disaster at sea, Odysseus and his men were driven in their ships through stormy seas for nine days and nights, until they came to the country of the "Junkies" (commonly known to all Classical Scholars, as the "Land of the Lotus Eaters.")

The inhabitants of this place had become absolute degenerates and completely given up the fight for 'Progress' and 'Civilization' (i.e. Wars, and Women, and Land!) and were perfectly content to simply lie around the beach, partaking of this honey sweet, lotus flower food, which destroyed all longings for Home-Status Symbols – and the Outside World!

"Say, man! Leave all that hassle! Enjoy a bit of this Lotus Flower, and switch on to a *new Psychodelic Experience!* This is the only way to endure Life *–Zonked out of your head!"* The Lotus Commune swarmed around the ship, making peace signs, and offering food.

But Odysseus thought of his two hundred acres of good arable land, his servants, slaves, live-stock, wife and child – and felt *no temptation whatsoever!*

"What would be the use of staying here with them?" he said to himself. "They quite obviously never had anything of value, *before* they came here! Whereas *I* am a King in Ithaca, and Society *Needs* me. I just can't leave all my responsibilities, to laze around in the sun, with this lot of No-Hopers!"

So Odysseus saved his men from ruin (because he needed them to man his ships) and promptly dragged the crew back on board again. Due to this timely action of his (and the fact that he had most of them tied up, so they *could not desert)* only a few of his sailors were lost.

However, the Sailors who had already become hooked on the Lotus Flower, wept and screamed loudly to return, but even they were eventually cured by a primitive form of 'Cold Turkey' Treatment, and the ships sailed on to the country inhabited by the **Cyclops Polyphemus.**

Polyphemus was a monster Cyclops who lived with other monster Cyclopes, in a special island which had been assigned to them by Zeus.

This land was a fertile area of good vineyards, corn fields, and fruit trees, where the Cyclopes grazed their large flocks of sheep and goats, and lived quietly but well, and in their spare time, they forged the 'Thunderbolts', which Zeus needed to use in order to maintain his 'Balance of Power' in the World.

These Cyclopes (who had only one eye each) were really very Anti-Zeus; but having been beaten soundly by him during the 'Creation Wars', they were forced to endure their exile, and to make the best of it.

Odysseus and his men though, did not even bother to think of who might be the owners of this country, but simply scrambled out of the boats, and made for a cave in which they found pens of sheep and goats, and vats of milk and cheese.

Naturally they helped themselves to the food, as they were never backward in coming forward (especially when it concerned nourishment) and were settling down to enjoy their stay, when all of a sudden, their *Host Appeared!*

Polyphemus was extremely annoyed to see these Greeks who had eaten his food without so much as a 'by your leave', and he became even more incensed when they started to whine, and to say that they were under the protection of Zeus, and therefore had the right to eat as much Cyclopian food as they liked!

"O.K." said Polyphemus. "If that's the way you want it – it's alright with me! You helped yourselves to *my food* – so I will help myself to *your food!*" and so saying, he began to pick up the Greeks, and eat them one at a time, without bothering to apply salt and pepper – or even a dash of ketchup!

This passion of Polyphemus' for fresh Greek Sailors, lasted for several days; with his selecting a couple for breakfast each morning, and again for dinner each night.

His mid-day meal however, he took in the fields with his flocks, and as making a sandwich of Greek Sailors presented him with a bit of a problem, he generally contented himself with only having milk and cheese for lunch. Possibly also, he was nutrition conscious, and knew that too much meat is bad for the digestive system, and is over-heating for the blood!

One evening, when the number of sailors had decreased to such an extent that Odysseus became worried in case he wouldn't have a large enough crew to see him home to Greece, he produced some wine, and offered it encouragingly to the Cyclops.

How Odysseus happened to have wine hidden on him all this time, is not explained in the mythology, but perhaps he was a secret drinker – along with all his other faults!

The wine must have been extremely good (or else Polyphemus was not used to alcohol) because after imbibing a couple of jars, he fell into a drunken slumber with his one eye tightly shut.

The Greeks then took a huge stake which they had previously sharpened and kept hidden for just such a moment, and having heated it, they drove it through the Cyclops' eye, blinding him as he lay dreaming in his liquor sodden sleep.

All this brutality seems to me, to have been *quite unnecessary!* For if the Greek wine had been *as good as it seems,* then Odysseus and his men could simply have left the cave while Polyphemus was drunkenly sleeping!

In fact the only thing they actually managed to accomplish by this ruthless action of theirs, was to awaken the Cyclops, who (though blinded, and in agonising pain) undertook to crawl to the front of the cave, and to sit with outstretched arms to make sure that none of the Greeks escaped.

Odysseus and his men then tied themselves beneath the bellies of the sheep and goats, and when the morning came, they passed out of the cave with the herd which Polyphemus always sent out to pasture at first light.

This whole story sounds extremely far-fetched, and it contains probably not one shred of truth (or is it grain?) as anyone with only the slightest acquaintance with sheep and goats will tell you. A sheep is quite a *haughty animal,* and doesn't take kindly to a man tying himself beneath its mid-rift, and would put up quite a show of discontent, should it be subjected to this type of indignity!

Probably the whole account of this incident with the Cyclops, is simply the product of a drinking bout which Odysseus had, and the resulting 'Delirium Tremens' following it. Alcoholics are known to suffer from over-heated imaginations – along with Poets and Returned Soldiers!

According to Odysseus however, they made their way down to the ships without being detected by the Giant, and even then, when they were all securely on board, and sailing out of the harbour, Odysseus just could not leave well enough alone, but had to be even more petty and vindictive.

Standing safely in the stern, he shouted back words to this effect. "Ha! Ha! You mighty Giant, you didn't manage to kill us after all! We were too smart for you! Yar! Boo! Sucks!" And he stuck out his tongue, and wriggled his ears in an extremely aggravating, and also perfectly useless manner – as Polyphemus, being now blind, couldn't see him anyway!

But the Cyclops heard Odysseus, and jumped up; threw a huge piece of the cliff in the direction of his voice, and only missed the last ship, by a cat's whisker!

And still, Odysseus, had to be a 'smart alec' and shout, "Cyclops! It is Odysseus, the Wrecker of Cities who put out your eye! *Do tell that, to anyone who should ask!"*

Such statements as these, are certainly not honourable (nor commendable!) and do nothing to enhance the reputation of Odysseus, but then we must remember that he was *only* a rough sailor, after all, and *not* really schooled in polite behaviour.

What Odysseus should have remembered (and would have, if he had ever stayed awake long enough during history lessons in school) was that *Poseidon* was the *father* of *Polyphemus,* and that this behaviour by Odysseus made him so mad, that he, Poseidon, tossed their boats around in a rage, and finally wrecked them in *another* country, far from Greece!

It is salutary to note that most of Odysseus' mis-adventures came about simply as the result of his abominable behaviour, and were completely *his own fault!* Perhaps the real message of all Greek Mythology is in fact, "How *NOT* to conduct yourself when travelling abroad!" – and perhaps it should be read with *only this precept in mind! (All Tourists please take note!)*

The country in which Odysseus and his men now came to rest, was that belonging to the Winds, and it was ruled over by kindly King Aeolus.

He was an extremely hospitable and generous old gentleman, and when they left, he gave Odysseus (as a form of farewell present) a leather sack tightly fastened, and into which, he had put every Storm Wind of the World.

This thoughtfulness on the part of **Aeolus** created excellent conditions for the sailors, but unfortunately they were just as stupid and badly brought-up as Odysseus, because they couldn't accept the sack graciously, but instead, wanted to undo it, in order to see what was inside.

The men had some crazy notion that there must be gold in it, and so, like Pandora with the box, they opened it, and out came all the storm winds of the world, which blew them off course, and around the oceans for many more days of suffering and sea-sickness (which were absolutely unnecessary) and could all have been avoided if they just had possessed even a few good manners to do as they were told. (And who says that Women are the Most Curious Creatures in the World? Odysseus' men certainly did not seem *to lack inquisitiveness!)*

The next country to which they finally came, belonged to the Laestrygons, a people of gigantic size, very ugly and quite bad-tempered, and who were cannibals to boot!

195

These sweet people destroyed *all* Odysseus' ships except for the one he was in (and which had not entered the port until last) and there before his very eyes was enacted the almost total extinction of his crew, as the **Laestrygons** chewed their way merrily through both wood and flesh.

With the sounds of weeping and wailing, and the gnashing of teeth, ringing in his ears (the 'gnashing', naturally enough, coming from the Laestrygons who were doing the feeding) Odysseus sailed away, leaving his comrades to be eaten, and sighed with relief that he wouldn't have a large pay-roll to make-up on the completion of his voyage!

Our pragmatic Captain now made his way to **Aeaea,** the realm of **Circe,** who was reputed to be the most beautiful and dangerous witch in the world, and who had a neat little trick for getting rid of guests who had become *Human Bores* – by turning them into *Animal Boars!*

She used to change men into swine; who then romped around eating acorns like swine, and rolled in the mud like swine, but who, all along, inside their heads, knew *THAT THEY WERE MEN!* – and were therefore *HORRIFIED AT THEIR DEGRADATION!*

Odysseus (realising something was wrong, but not realising exactly what that something was) sent a spy, to watch what was happening to all his men who had entered Circe's house and who then mysteriously disappeared. The spy then returned and reported this strange and horrible tale of swinish **Metamorphosis,** whereupon the brave Captain set off himself to personally deal with this woman, who was making pigs of his men!

(Strangely enough it never seems to have occurred to Odysseus that it could have been *his men* who were *making pigs of themselves,* by eating and drinking everything they could find in Circe's Bar and Tavern!)

As this intrepid sailor approached the diabolical den, Hermes suddenly appeared, and gave him a magic herbal drink in order to immunize him against Circe's deadly spells.

Therefore, when Odysseus faced Circe; drank her potion; remained his *well-mannered self;* and *didn't start* snorting around the place, and rooting in the larder; the Enchantress was amazed – and even delighted!

It seems that Circe was getting sick of the sight of pigs, and having finally found a man who could hold his liquor without making a fool of himself, she fell madly in love with Odysseus, and was ony too happy to bring his men back to their original forms – give them all a cup of black coffee each – and sober them up in general!

(Probably this section of the Odyssey was simply an excuse for some fairly heavy moralizing on the condition and state of man whilst under the influence of strong drink, and Hermes had obviously supplied Odysseus with some type of early anti – 'hang-over' drug, which would make a fortune if it were marketed in the world today, and which would save a large section of Humanity (including the author) from a great deal of despair on the 'morning after', the 'night before'!)

In between dunking drunken pigs of men under cold water faucets, Circe told them what they must do, in order to eventually get home to Greece.

Firstly they had to cross the river Ocean, and beach their ship on Persephone's shore where lay the entrance to the dark realm of Hades.

Then Odysseus had to go down and find the spirit of the Prophet Teiresias, who had been a Holy man of some importance in Thebes and who would then tell Odysseus how to actually get back to Greece.

The main problem though, was that in order to get the ghost of Teiresias to appear, they had to kill some sheep, and to fill a pit with their blood, so that the ghost could come up, quench his thirst a little, and then get on with the job of telling them what they wanted to know.

It appeared that *ALL GHOSTS* had an irresistible craving to drink *BLOOD,* and this highly florid story, likely as not, began the myth of Dracula, which was to tingle many a person's spine, and to make so much money for Hollywood in the years to come.

Circe warned them also, that *all* the ghosts of Hades would come rushing up to the pit, but that Odysseus must draw his sword and keep them away, until **Teiresias** had drunk his fill, and spoken to him. She added that it was absolutely no use trying to get them to accept the odd glass of cognac, or rum, as *ONLY* blood would do, and that ghosts could *tell the difference,* a mile away!

So shivering and shaking, they turned the prow of their only remaining ship towards Erebus, where Hades ruled. Once there, they landed, dug their trench; killed a sheep; filled the pit with blood; and stood waiting for the dead to come forth for a drink.

Odysseus remembered Circe's words, and formed the Dead into a queue (which would have made even a London Bus Conductor proud) and they all had to wait patiently until Teiresias came and had wet his whistle, and was ready to engage in a little light conversation.

It might be of interest to the Reader to note (there again it might not – but I shall tell you anyway!) that this Teiresias was the blind prophet of Thebes who had foretold of the birth and greatness of Hercules. As he had also been such a prophet of doom regarding many a Royal House in Greece, few had mourned him on his passing. (No one *really* likes to have a kill-joy around the place – no matter how intelligent he is!)

Teiresias told them that they would be journeying to an island on which lived the oxen of the Sun, and that above all else, they must be careful *not to harm* these beautiful beasts. (Livestock were very important to the ancient people, as they were the greatest source and outward symbol of all individual wealth. A cow in the back-yard was as good as a Credit Card in those days, and far more useful, as anyone who has ever tried to eat a bank-note will tell you!)

Furthermore, the Seer warned Odysseus, that when he reached home, he would find trouble waiting for him; and with these cryptic words, Teiresias disappeared, and the other ghosts took over, and came to have a sup.

Odysseus' mother then stepped up and claimed the head of the queue (as after all it was her son who was running the soup kitchen) and Achilles, and Ajax, and all the other Spectres had no choice but to agree with her – even if there was some mumbling about how long they'd had to wait already.

The ghosts kept filing past and saying 'Howdy', and there never seemed to be an end to these ghastly thirst-driven, dypsomaniac 'Shades'. And Odysseus and his men decided to beat it before the 'Gorgon' or 'Medusa' should suddenly appear, and strike them all to stone.

"Bye-bye, Ma! It's been nice seeing you, and I'll give your love to everyone at home. Sorry, but I've got to rush now!" shouted Odysseus, making for the ship.

"That's a good son for you! Always has been, and always will be! Nothing too good for his mother, and nothing too much trouble! Many a mother would be proud to have a son like mine!" and bending down smuggly in maternal conceit, Odysseus' mother took another transfusion, as her son sailed off into the mists, hoping to heaven that he'd *never have to see the old hag again!*

"Why is it" said Odysseus to himself. "Why is it that she never seems to understand that I'm a *grown man?* Always treating me like a child! *Silly old fool!"*

Odysseus was so disturbed from this encounter with his mother that he lost his concentration, and took an unnecessary risk when sailing past the island of the 'Sirens' on his way to Greece.

These 'Sirens' happened to be marvellous singing women, with sensuous lilting voices, who dwelt above an island of rocks, and from whose cliffs hung the mouldering skeletons of men who had been lured to their death, while pursuing these golden sounds, and fascinating women.

Odysseus made in his men put wax in their ears, so that they wouldn't hear the voices at all. But himself, he had tied to a mast (so strongly that he could not break the bonds) and he listened to their song which promised the knowledge and wisdom of all things, and which filled every listener's heart with longing.

Odysseus, because of the ropes, was unable to satisfy this longing – and that was probably a good thing too, because how many people have ever made a fortune pursuing Wisdom and Knowledge?

The Philosophers, Creators, and Inventors of this world may *spur on progress,* but they generally die *without a penny to their names,* and Socrates' descendants would probably be much happier today, if their illustrious ancestor had marketed Coca-Cola – instead of directing Man in search of his Soul!

On and on they travelled, through the passage between **Scylla** and **Charybdis** which had caused so much trouble to the Argonauts, and which would at a later date cause trouble to the Founder of Rome – Aeneas.

They survived these dangerous waters with only six crew lost (due entirely to the intervention of Athena who was constantly hovering around, and urging Odysseus and his men ever forward) and finally disembarked at the Island of the Sun (which might have been Delos, the birthplace of Apollo, as the God of Arts was also known as the Sun God, with whom he was often confused in the period after the Old Gods had been dispossessed.)

At the **Island of the Sun,** Odysseus got a sudden fit of piety, or was re-born, or something of the sort; because he decided to sit down by himself and to pray (a thing which he should obviously have done years before, and which coming to at this late stage in his career, seemed rather senseless. But then even the worst of us seem to feel the need of a little religion in later life when we catch sight of the "Great Leveler" and "Grim Reaper" hanging around outside the door!)

The Crew, by now however, were pretty discontented – and *very hungry!* So they decided to do something by themselves to rectify matters pertaining to their physical selves.

"Why should we sit around starving, while that stupid idiot sits communing with the Gods? We haven't received a penny for our troubles all this time, and he's been enjoying himself with all the women we've met along the way, and *nagging* and *castigating* us if we so much as *sniffed* in the direction of a pair of dainty sandals! Now he wants us to *starve to death* – in order not to pay us, when we get back home to Greece!"

So they took decisive action and killed an oxe; barbecued it; and ate their fill, like hearty men (little knowing that this was to be their *last supper!)*

As soon as the ship had left the port, a terrible storm arose (which proves the Gods are not joking when they say that people shouldn't eat their livestock!) and everyone on board was drowned except of course *Odysseus* – who floated on the waves in sanctimonious splendour, to land on Calypso's Island; where he lived in upright purity for many years, defending his honour with vigorous determination.

"I'm a poor man, but I'm virtuous!" Odysseus said to **Calypso.** "Don't even ask me to do such a thing!" he cried. "You know you'll only use me for your pleasure, and then throw me in the gutter! If once I lose my honour, what future is there for me? Who would want me after you had had your way, and despoiled me?"

"Go on with you!" replied Calypso. "We haven't even got any gutters on this island! It's something I never got round to seeing to–I don't know why!"

And she went off grumbling to herself, to check her Magic Spells Ready – Reference Book, on how to trap Intrepid Males who proved difficult to seduce.

So the Odyssey of Odysseus ended, and everyone in the Court breathed a sigh of relief, for if the ending wasn't exactly a happy one, then it wasn't a tragic one either!

(And most probably they were also sighing from relief that

he'd finally finished the story which had kept them all from getting a good night's sleep.)

The King decided to get rid of Odysseus as quickly as possible, because with such a story-teller around, no one would ever do any work whatsoever. And, he the King, personally saw to it that Odysseus was despatched to a ship (with plenty of food and drink) and the Hero stretched himself out, and fell into a deep contented slumber.

When the ship arrived in Greece, the Phaeacian sailors simply unloaded Odysseus (still fast asleep) with all his belongings, and left him on the beach, while they quietly departed. They were probably rather afraid that if they woke him up, he would begin talking again, and wouldn't stop – and then they'd never be able to get home in time for dinner!

"I'd rather listen to that fellow for a week than a fortnight", they whispered to each other, while casting off. "He'd drive you to drink after awhile!"

Odysseus finally awoke; but when he did so, hadn't the faintest idea were he was.

Then Athena appeared, told him that he was home in Ithaca; and brought him up to date on all that had been going on his house while his back had been turned; how Penelope was beating off suitors with one hand, and sewing shrouds with the other; and how Telemachus was becoming Muscle – bound and constipated, from sitting in the cellar all day long.

This shroud incidentally, was supposed to be for Odysseus' father, whom Penelope had kept hoping might die, and whom she had used as an excuse to keep her male courtiers dangling. She had announced to her suitors that she couldn't marry any of them until she had finished this bit of home-shroud-making; and that then, with a clear conscience, she would be able to turn her mind to fashioning a wedding gown for herself; in order to marry one of them!

But Odysseus' father never did die (although he kept promising to!) and Penelope kept tearing out her work every night, because she was displeased with the cut and line of the thing; and the suitors got fed-up and said they couldn't wait any longer; that she'd have to hurry and make up her mind! and that they'd marry her, even in her apron strings; as they didn't much care *what she looked like!*

(NOTE TO FEMALE READERS. When a man says that he doesn't care what you look like, it is very likely to be *true* – and means that he's much more interested in your *bank balance,* than in your *face!* – So Beware!!)

Simultaneously upon Odysseus' arrival in Ithaca, Athena arranged to bring Telemachus home again from Sparta, so father and son were finally re-united, and together they made plans for getting rid of the suitors.

Odysseus entered his own home disguised as a beggar, only to find that Penelope had at long last come to the end of her tether, and had therefore decided to marry the richest and strongest drunkard in her lounge room. Therefore she had told them all to give her tokens of their sincerity, in order for her to determine which one had the thickest chequebook!

After taking most of their money, Penelope then produced an old bow and arrow of Odysseus', and said that whoever could string the bow, could claim her hand. – Then she went up to her bed for a nap, because the whole affair was making her a nervous wreck, and moreover, she'd had a hard enough day, just counting their filthy lucre!

Naturally none of the suitors could string the bow, except the beggar (who was really Odysseus, if you remember) and having strung it, he shot and killed the whole assembly of scrounging lay-abouts-with the help of Telemachus, who charged around knocking them in the aisles with his biceps!

The only person that Odysseus spared in his revenge, was the Bard, who said he had been taught by the Gods to sing divinely of the exploits of men, and so Odysseus decided to keep him around for further use; in case he ever needed anyone to sing about him and his Odyssey!

(In this part of the Odyssey we have a nice little bit of propaganda for writers and poets in general, and it vouch-saves them from persecution from the mortals – by order of the Gods! Strangely enough, nobody seems to follow these directions nowadays, as poets and writers are always the first ones to be thrown into prison everywhere, whenever the 'Establishment' feels a little cranky, and out-of-sorts.)

Then the old faithful servant of the household, who had known Odysseus from when he was a babe, was sent up to awaken Penelope, who was most annoyed at being disturbed in the midst of her siesta (though how she could have slept with that rumpus going on, makes one wonder, as killing 574 people is bound to be a *noisy business!*)

Penelope didn't believe that the beggar waiting below, was her long lost husband (memory and time always play tricks on a person) for she remembered Odysseus as a young, handsome, fit and virile specimen of male pulchritude; and had some trouble recognising this balding, middle-aged gent, with a paunch, and a weather beaten face.

Telemachus got quite annoyed with his mother, when she kept repeating, "Is it really you? It can't be!"

"I tell you it is!" said Telemachus, in exasperation.

"Never mind your mother!" Odysseus said, and laughed, for he had quite a way with the ladies; as has been shown by the way he manoeuvered Athena to please himself, and get him home.

"This is the way of women!" said Odysseus, wisely. "They never once want, whatever it is that they've found! She'll get over this strangeness in time, don't you fret! But for now, I'm ordering a quiet, candle–lit supper for the two of us, and Telemachus can go back to the cellar for the evening. Penelope, you and I will have some music, and dance and enjoy ourselves. It's time we got to know each other again!"

And they did. And that was that. And the Odyssey of Odysseus was finally over. And for once, in Greek Mythology, *everyone lived Happily Ever After!*

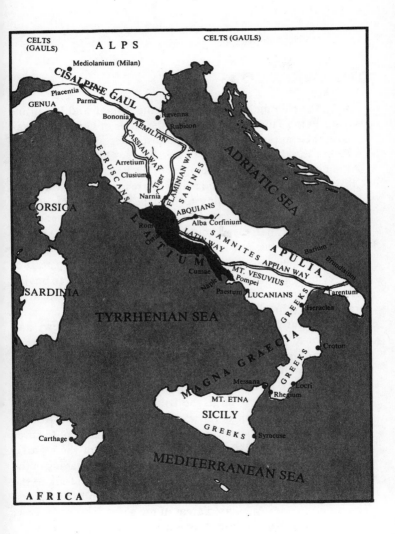

CHAPTER X

THE GREEK GODS TODAY

With the coming of Christianity in the Roman and Byzantine Worlds in the Third Century A.D., the Gods of Olympus began to lose their appeal – or *seemed* to lose their appeal.

People may have continued to worship the Gods in the privacy of their own hearts, but the temples to the Pagan Deities became Christian Churches; and their statues were removed to Museums of chilling cold, more fitting to be called mausoleums. Other works of art were even created, in order to honour another group of people not half as glamourous, nor as exciting, as the Olympians had been.

Business men began to form Lodges and Guilds, instead of congregating at the home of Hermes; and women took to buying pills and potions, and visiting massage parlours; instead of praying at Aphrodite's temple.

Consequently the Gods moved on to pastures new; and existed for a short, unhappy time, in the Holy Roman Empire, masquarading as Christian Saints! But the Holy Roman Empire was only 'small potatoes' after what they had been used to; and the call of 'Pax Britannia' sounded loud in their ears.

But no matter how large the British Empire was, it didn't really suit all of them, because, unlike the Greek and Roman Empires, the British never catered to every taste, and could never have been accused of 'Catholicity' in any sense of the word!

The Olympians gradually split up. The majority staying in the Empire in which the sun never set, but some of them took to the Colonies (as being more congenial for work) and still others, emigrated to non–Anglicized areas of the globe. This period was a most unsettling time for all of them!

Athena however, elected to stay in England, and in consequence received a new name – Britannia. She took over Poseidon's job as well, and took up standing on guard in the English Channel in order to keep out all undesirable foreign influences. *(Which really meant everyone who wasn't English!)* In her leisure hours, she marched around humming "Rule Britannia", and "Land of Hope and Glory" to herself, posed for statues to be placed in parks and gardens in London, and greatly inspired all pictures and objects de guerre for the British War Museum.

Poseidon himself became re-named Davy Jones, and was sent to stay deep down in the depths of the sea to await the bodies of dead sailors. He found himself pretty busy in every century, and really didn't mind about the loss of Status in Nomenclature. Besides which, during crossings of the Equatorial Line, he came in for great ceremonial respect, which was almost as good as in the good old days.

Aphrodite though, never could endure the prudish British atmosphere, so she went off to France, a country in which she felt more at home, and in which she held a wider influence. Besides her stock-in-trade 'Love', she was able to dabble in a little revolutionary activity, and having gained some wisdom from her dreadful experiences as Troy, was able to offer more helpful inspiration during the upheavals of 1789 to 1871; and paintings of her carrying Tri-colours through the streets of Paris, can be viewed nowadays in the Louvre.

Hermes, like Athena, stayed on in Britain, and having donned a bowler hat (and pin-stripe suit) and having adopted an umbrella instead of his customary wand, made his way to Threadneedle Street, the Bank of England, and the Stock-Market. There was a great deal of commerce in the British Empire (more than enough to satisfy him) and the East India Company was especially to his liking.

Hephaestus also stayed in England, and helped to form Trade Unions and various Craftsmen's Guilds at the time of the

Industrial Revolution, and aided the 'Establishment' greatly, by making sure, that the workers, *never* got out of hand, and *never* had a *real revolution!*

Apollo, like Aphrodite, never could stand the English climate of practicality and commerce, and having flit here and there, took to living in Ireland, where he found the people to be extremely sympathetic, but that the rain got on his nerves (also the political problem). With regret, he departed, and journeyed to Italy, where from the time of the Renaissance onwards, he found the most congenial atmosphere for him both climatically and artistically. In Apollo we have a fine example of First Generation Immigrant children who feel that they have to return to their 'Roots'. In Ireland he had enjoyed the experience of being once more around the Celts of Ancient Switzerland and France, but he still preferred to be closer to Rome, "The Mother of the Gods".

Hera and Hestia, on the other hand, were quite happy to settle down in Britain, where the Victorian Era especially suited their particular talents for raising large families of conservative citizens, and for providing all the necessary elements for the production of frustrated females.

Zeus, Pluto, and Ares, never stayed in any one spot for long, but took to wandering Europe and dividing their loyalties, and their time, with *every European Power* – and even with some Europeans who had no power at all!

Artemis, the Loner and Individualist, left for the New World of America as soon as she was able, and commenced trapping for a living. And for companionship she spent her time with the Indians – whose company she found more progressive, and less hypocritical than the Whiteman's.

Dionysos meanwhile, had an overwhelming success among the poor of *every country,* and temples sprung up to him everywhere! Especially in Ireland, where his converts exceeded the number of *all his previous worshippers throughout the past ages!* People there had decided that if they couldn't resurrect

Athena Strikes Again! – This time as Britannia.

themselves one way, then they'd do it another –and that it was better to 'Drink' – than to 'Think!'

But despite all these changes and moves, the Gods were really far from happy, and missed having a place of their very own, and a definite settled area from which they could all work, and which they could all regard as "home".

In 1948 they found that permanent base when they all managed to come together under one roof so to speak, and that roof being the 'Stars and Stripes of the U.S.A.'

Aphrodite went directly to Hollywood, where she now directs the movie business, and promotes the 'American Dream'. She also runs a chain of Beauty Salons on the side, and is a world-wide distributor of a famous Cosmetics Monopoly.

Hera immediately joined the 'Daughters of the Revolution', and other patriotic married women's guilds, and has been responsible for the legislation which brought about the Community Property Divorce Settlement Act in California. She also puts out an 'Agony Column', which is syndicated nation wide, and in which she offers advice on how to skin your husband in the divorce courts, and how to make the most out of a broken marriage!

Hermes found a permanent home in Wall Street, from which he directs world wide agencies and companies, and, despite inflation, is not running short of cash. (After all, he is the one who actually plans when the Depression is to begin!)

Pluto fell on his feet in Texas, where he controls the oil wealth, and besides this, also runs a successful Undertaking Racket in Los Angeles, which is (at present) the most modern in the world. He also naturally secured the Government Contract for handling all the shipments and transfers of Overseas Dead (which enterprise has been quite substantial at certain periods, as for instance in the 1960's!)

Apollo left the Arts entirely (as he decided it was not a paying proposition in the 20th Century) and went into Space Travel at Kennedy Centre, after a suitable period of Re-Training.

210

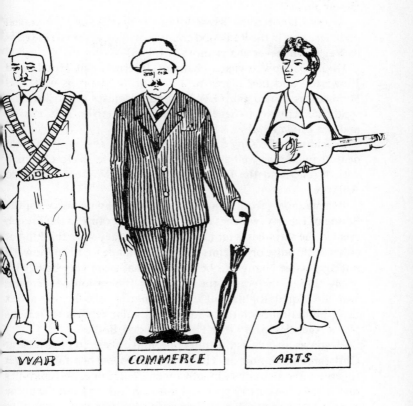

The Progeny of the Olympic System live on.

Everything had changed with the advance of the Technological Era, and Apollo decided it was better to be Re-deployed, than Un-employed!

Artemis ignored the whole lot of the Family, and has stayed on in Oregon, in the Redwood country, with occasional side trips to Vegas whenever she is short of bread!

Dionysos how owns a chain of International Hotels and Breweries, and has shares in a soft drink chain as well, and Hephaestus joined the G.W.U., and organises all strikes and syndicate activities (whenever it is convenient to both *the Bosses,* and *the Union Leaders,* of course!)

Poseidon is the King of the Sea once more, and enjoys a great deal of public, as well as private respect, as he is closely allied with NATO and the Defense Aims of the Western Seaboard Alliance.

Athena, apart from mouthing off about having posed for the Statue of Liberty (which is a downright lie, because as the French created the statue, it is far more likely that they were thinking of either Aphrodite or Artemis when it was made – and anyhow it's not aggressive enough to be Athena!) has been very busy with many things, including, the Women's Liberation Movement, and the Equal Rights Bill in Washington. She is also a Sex Descrimination Monitor, and sends regular reports to various News Agencies, and other Public Minded Bodies.

Hestia as always, is the quiet one, and only shows her nose at Christmas time, and on Thanksgiving Days when families get together. She also edits a lot of women's magazines and compiles marvellous cooking recipes and hints on how to keep the home clean and attractive on a shoe-string budget, and on how to maintain a stable influence in the house, in other to produce psychologically sound American Youth.

Ares is permanently employed in the Pentagon, although he sometimes commutes to Moscow as well – (it's always best to be on the safe side)! Besides which, consulations with the 'Enemy' *are always advisable!* And anyway, Ares doesn't really mind which side he is working on – so long as he is working!

The Captain of the Gods, old Zeus himself, took to the White House and the Senate as if they had been made for him (as indeed they possibly were). His symbol the Eagle, is used in the U.S.A. as it was in Rome and Greece, only to differentiate, it is called the "Bald-Headed Eagle". Zeus of course is not concerned with trifles. He knows that really it is just the same old bird!

The Lesser Gods are scattered around the globe with the Headquarters of their Organisations in either New York, or Washington, and although their temples are not always *obvious,* you will see them if you look *carefully enough.*

It only takes a second to de-cant the stale wine of your mind, and unscale your unseeing eyes, and then you will observe that *the Olympians, are all around you* – just as happy and contented, respected and worshipped, as they ever were!

THE END

Zeus: The God of Gods and People

The Throne of Zeus (Mt Olympus)

Mount Olympus

The two most impressive peaks of Olympus. The Throne of Zeus (left) and Myticas (right)

Zeus

Zeus and Andiope: *by Corregio*

The Gold-and-Ivory
statue of Athena

Amphora in red figure
technique depicting Athena

Apollo fighting Centaurs

Kneeling Aphrodite

Aphrodite, Pan and Eros

The Birth of Aphrodite: *by Botticelli*

The Triumph of Aphrodite: *by Francesco Pontesti*

The Graces scattering flowers. Aphrodite in the middle

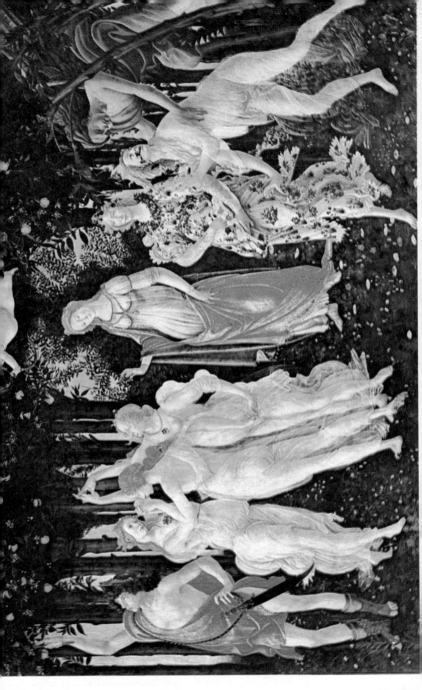

Aphrodite Aris and little Satyrs

The Three Graces: *by Botticelli*

Statue of Demeter of Cnidos

Hermis holding infant Dionysus: *by Praxiteles*

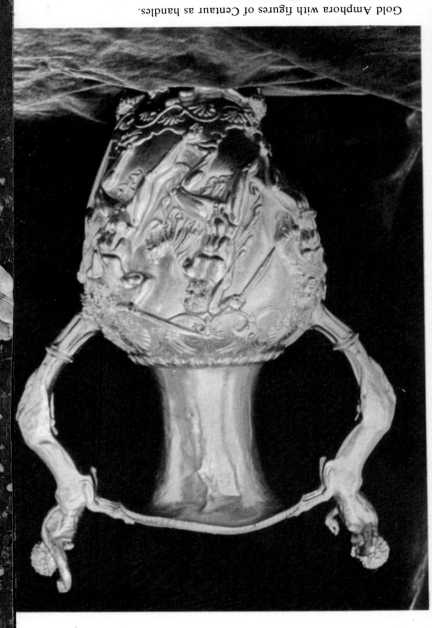

Gold Amphora with figures of Centaur as handles.
Attic petite in red figure technique. Paris being promised Aphrodite by Er

Attic Amphora: The Abduction of Hippodamia: *by Pelops*

Apollo and Daphne: *by Andrea Appiani*

Attic Krater in red-figure technique: Dionysus, the patron of the Theatre, in the arms of Ariadne

Calyx-Crater showing Artemis getting ready to shoot

Gold Amphora with figures of Centaur as handles.

Attic pelite in red figure technique. Paris being promised Aphrodite by Eros

Attic Amphora: The Abduction of Hippodamia: *by Pelops*

Apollo and Daphne: *by Andrea Appiani*